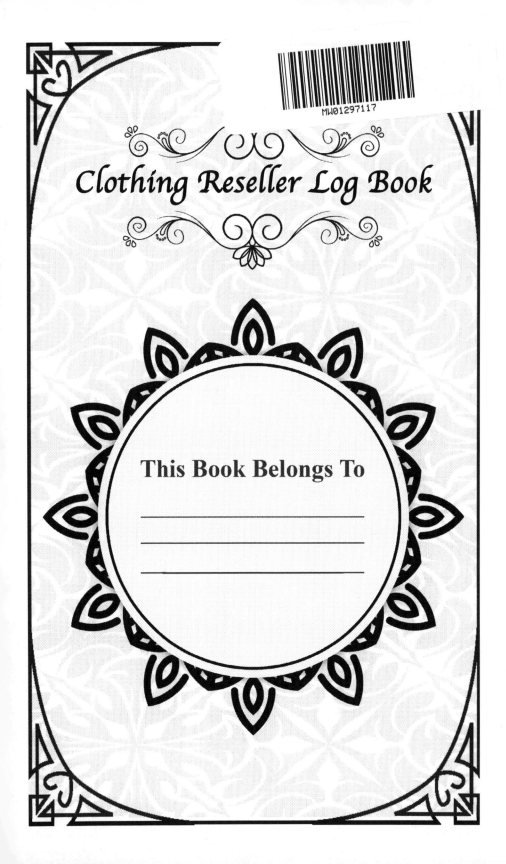

Clothing Reseller Log Book

FOLLOW ME ON INSTAGRAM

SCAN ME

Don't forget to visit: www.QueenThrift.com

Sign up to be notified of any free giveaways, new logbooks, and future updates to the books!

Thank you for your support!

Disclaimer:

I am not a financial professional, and the information provided here is only for general informational purposes. The content of this book is based on general knowledge and should not be considered financial advice.

Small business tax regulations can be complex and subject to change. It is crucial to consult with a qualified financial professional or tax advisor to obtain personalized advice tailored to your specific business situation.

While efforts are made to provide accurate and up-to-date information, I cannot guarantee the content's completeness, accuracy, or relevance. Therefore, seek professional advice to ensure that any decisions regarding small business tax deductions are appropriate for your unique circumstances. Using this book, you acknowledge that I am not a financial professional, and any reliance on the information provided is at your own risk. Consultation with a qualified financial professional is strongly advised for small business tax deductions.

Copyright © 2019, 2023 by Gianeska Publishing, Inc. dba QueenThrift.com

All rights reserved. No part of this publication may be reproduced, distributed, or transmitted in any form or by any means, including photocopying, recording, or other electronic or mechanical methods, without the prior written permission of the publisher, except in the case of brief quotations embodied in critical reviews and certain other noncommercial uses permitted by copyright law

Boost Your eBay Business:
A Guide to Setting and Achieving Your Business Goals.

Setting and achieving business goals is a powerful strategy to drive success. In this guide, we'll delve into the why and how to stay on track with your listing goals and share tips on staying on track with your business objectives.

1. Define Your Objectives
Before delving into listings, take a moment to define your overall business objectives. Are you aiming to increase sales, expand your product range, or reach a specific revenue target? Having a clear vision provides a foundation for your listing goals.

2. Break Down Your Goals
Rather than setting a broad target, break it down into smaller, achievable goals. For instance, consider listing a certain number of items per week or introducing a new product category every month. Breaking down goals makes them more manageable and less overwhelming.

3. Consistency is Key
Consistent listing is crucial for building buyer trust and improving your eBay store's visibility. Create a regular listing schedule to keep your store active and engaging. Consistency not only attracts potential customers but also retains existing ones.

4. Quality Over Quantity
While setting goals, emphasize the quality of your listings. Accurate product descriptions, high-quality images, and competitive pricing are essential for attracting and retaining customers. Focus on creating listings that stand out in content and presentation.

5. Leverage eBay Tools
Explore the various seller tools offered by eBay to streamline the listing process. These tools can significantly optimize your workflow and enhance your store's visibility, from bulk editing to promoted listings. Please familiarize yourself with these features to maximize their impact on your business.

Pick one or more goals from each category to include in your Weekly Plan

Daily goals	<ul><li>List items with profit goal amount—for example, $100 profit daily. List five items with at least $20 profit every single day.</li><li>Prep items to photograph the next day.</li><li>Hang and air out all items brought from sourcing. Launder and clean what needs to be cleaned. Inspect all items and discard damaged goods.</li><li>(Optional) 20 Min promote your store. Share on Poshmark, twitter, Instagram, Pinterest, Facebook, etc.</li></ul>
Weekly Goals	<ul><li>Log Sales for the week (Weekly Plan sheets)</li><li>Run sale. Offer previous buyers a discount coupon.</li><li>Identify one business aspect to improve: Inventory management, sourcing, listing faster.</li><li>10 Min Prune Store. What needs to be price reduced to sell? Donated?</li><li>Look at store sales through rate and traffic stats.</li></ul>
Monthly Goals	<ul><li>Go through physical inventory area and clear out old unsold items. Setup cheap auction or donate.</li><li>Establish relationship with your sourcing options. Make contacts at local stores to secure inventory.</li><li>Research your chosen categories for more product opportunities. Go through sold listings.</li><li>Implement new selling strategies, promotions, keywords, photography, inventory management. Never stop learning.</li></ul>

Notes:

Monthly Seller Account Reconciliation Instructions

Total Income from sales:	Gather all your monthly statements from all the selling books you currently have sales on. Add all the gross sales in here.
Taxes Collected by books:	Tax regulations can be complex and subject to change. By maintaining a log, you can stay compliant with tax laws, providing a transparent record of taxes paid, which is essential for audits and regulatory compliance.
Gross Profit:	Subtract the tax amount from the Gross Sales. This is your gross profit, which you will have to deduct from your expenses.
Marketplace Fees:	Add up your total fees paid this month, which should be reflected on your monthly statement.
Cost of Goods Sold (COGS)	Amount spent on current inventory. How much did you spend sourcing this month? If none, write Zero.
Shipping Expenses:	If you use an outside company like Pirate Ship to ship your packages, get a monthly statement to obtain your total. Otherwise, check your sales book statement for a separate shipping charge.
Refunds	Tracking refunds ensures the accuracy of your financial records. It allows you to account for both revenue and expenses accurately.
Business Expenses:	Gas, Tolls, Apps, Wages, Assistants, supplies, etc. Keep good records and receipts of all business expenses.
Net Profit	Subtract your Total Expenses from your Gross Profit.
Miles Deductions:	Businesses can deduct certain vehicle expenses on their tax returns, and mileage is a common deductible expense. Makes it easy comes tax time to include this deductions with your business taxes.

By keeping detailed records, you can easily track your business's trajectory, identify patterns, and make informed decisions. This financial transparency enables you to pinpoint areas for improvement, optimize spending, and strategically plan for the future.

Weekly Plan

Week: _____

MONDAY

TUESDAY

WED

THURSDAY

FRIDAY

SATURDAY

SUNDAY

Goals This Week

- ☐ Listing:_____
- ☐ Sourcing_____
- ☐ _____
- ☐ _____
- ☐ _____

Sales This Week

- ❖ _____
- ❖ _____
- ❖ _____

Improvements

- ➢ _____
- ➢ _____
- ➢ _____

Expenses:

- ➢ _____
- ➢ _____
- ➢ _____
- ➢ _____

Notes:

"Success is not something that just happens.. Success is learned, success is practiced, and then it is shared…"
Sparky Anderson

Weekly Plan

Week: _____

MONDAY

TUESDAY

WED

THURSDAY

FRIDAY

SATURDAY

SUNDAY

Goals This Week
- ☐ Listing:_____
- ☐ Sourcing_____
- ☐ _____
- ☐ _____
- ☐ _____

Sales This Week
- ❖ _____
- ❖ _____
- ❖ _____

Improvements
- ➢ _____
- ➢ _____
- ➢ _____

Expenses:
- ➢ _____
- ➢ _____
- ➢ _____
- ➢ _____

Notes:

"Success is the sum of small efforts, repeated day in and day out..."
Robert Collier

Weekly Plan

Week: _____

MONDAY

TUESDAY

WED

THURSDAY

FRIDAY

SATURDAY

SUNDAY

Goals This Week
- ☐ Listing:_____
- ☐ Sourcing_____
- ☐ _____
- ☐ _____
- ☐ _____

Sales This Week
- ❖ _____
- ❖ _____
- ❖ _____

Improvements
- ➢ _____
- ➢ _____
- ➢ _____

Expenses:
- ➢ _____
- ➢ _____
- ➢ _____
- ➢ _____

Notes:

Action is the foundational key to all success.
Pablo Picasso

Weekly Plan

Week: _____

MONDAY

TUESDAY

WED

THURSDAY

FRIDAY

SATURDAY

SUNDAY

Goals This Week

- ❏ Listing:_____
- ❏ Sourcing_____
- ❏ _____
- ❏ _____
- ❏ _____

Sales This Week

- ❖ _____
- ❖ _____
- ❖ _____

Improvements

- ➢ _____
- ➢ _____
- ➢ _____

Expenses:

- ➢ _____
- ➢ _____
- ➢ _____
- ➢ _____

Notes:

*"The Creation of a thousand forests
In in one acorn."*
Ralph Waldo Emerson

Monthly Seller Account Reconciliation

INCOME	Month: 20___
Total Income from Sales:	$
Taxes collected by books:	$
Gross Profit (Total Sales minus Taxes)	$

EXPENSES	
Marketplaces Fees:	$
Cost of Goods Sold (COGS):	$
Shipping Expenses:	$
Storage/Rent:	$
Refunds:	$
Business Expenses (Apps, Software, etc.)	$
Other:	
Total Expenses for the Month:	$

PROFIT / LOSS	Month: 20___
Net Profit = Gross Profit − Total Expenses	$
Net Profit Last Month:	$

Miles Deduction This Month: _____ Miles x $_____ / Per Mile =	$

Weekly Plan

Week: _____

MONDAY

TUESDAY

WED

THURSDAY

FRIDAY

SATURDAY

SUNDAY

Goals This Week
- ❏ Listing:_____
- ❏ Sourcing_____
- ❏ _____
- ❏ _____
- ❏ _____

Sales This Week
- ❖ _____
- ❖ _____
- ❖ _____

Improvements
- ➢ _____
- ➢ _____
- ➢ _____

Expenses:
- ➢ _____
- ➢ _____
- ➢ _____
- ➢ _____

Notes:

The mind is everything. What you think, you become. ~ **Gautama Buddha.**

Weekly Plan

Week: _____

MONDAY

TUESDAY

WED

THURSDAY

FRIDAY

SATURDAY

SUNDAY

Goals This Week
- ❏ Listing:_____
- ❏ Sourcing_____
- ❏ _____
- ❏ _____
- ❏ _____

Sales This Week
- ❖ _____
- ❖ _____
- ❖ _____

Improvements
- ➢ _____
- ➢ _____
- ➢ _____

Expenses:
- ➢ _____
- ➢ _____
- ➢ _____
- ➢ _____

Notes:

For success, attitude is equally as important as ability.
Walter Scott

Weekly Plan

Week: _____

MONDAY

TUESDAY

WED

THURSDAY

FRIDAY

SATURDAY

SUNDAY

Goals This Week
- ☐ Listing:_____
- ☐ Sourcing_____
- ☐ _____
- ☐ _____
- ☐ _____

Sales This Week
- ❖ _____
- ❖ _____
- ❖ _____

Improvements
- ➢ _____
- ➢ _____
- ➢ _____

Expenses:
- ➢ _____
- ➢ _____
- ➢ _____
- ➢ _____

Notes:

Wise men speak because they have something to say; Fools because they have to say something.
Plato

Weekly Plan

Week: _____

MONDAY

TUESDAY

WED

THURSDAY

FRIDAY

SATURDAY

SUNDAY

Goals This Week

- ☐ Listing:_____
- ☐ Sourcing_____
- ☐ _____
- ☐ _____
- ☐ _____

Sales This Week

- ❖ _____
- ❖ _____
- ❖ _____

Improvements

- ➢ _____
- ➢ _____
- ➢ _____

Expenses:

- ➢ _____
- ➢ _____
- ➢ _____
- ➢ _____

Notes:

The greatest test of courage on earth is to bear defeat without losing heart.
Robert Green Ingersoll

Monthly Seller Account Reconciliation

INCOME	Month: 20___
Total Income from Sales:	$
Taxes collected by books:	$
Gross Profit (Total Sales minus Taxes)	$

EXPENSES	
Marketplaces Fees:	$
Cost of Goods Sold (COGS):	$
Shipping Expenses:	$
Storage/Rent:	$
Refunds:	$
Business Expenses (Apps, Software, etc.)	$
Other:	
Total Expenses for the Month:	$

PROFIT / LOSS	Month: 20___
Net Profit = Gross Profit – Total Expenses	$
Net Profit Last Month:	$

Miles Deduction This Month: _____ Miles x $_____ / Per Mile =	$

Weekly Plan

Week: _____

MONDAY

TUESDAY

WED

THURSDAY

FRIDAY

SATURDAY

SUNDAY

Goals This Week

- ☐ Listing:_____
- ☐ Sourcing_____
- ☐ _____
- ☐ _____
- ☐ _____

Sales This Week

- ❖ _____
- ❖ _____
- ❖ _____

Improvements

- ➢ _____
- ➢ _____
- ➢ _____

Expenses:

- ➢ _____
- ➢ _____
- ➢ _____
- ➢ _____

Notes:

Experience is the teacher of all things.
Julius Caesar

Weekly Plan

Week: _____

MONDAY

TUESDAY

WED

THURSDAY

FRIDAY

SATURDAY

SUNDAY

Goals This Week
- ☐ Listing:_____
- ☐ Sourcing_____
- ☐ _____
- ☐ _____
- ☐ _____

Sales This Week
- ❖ _____
- ❖ _____
- ❖ _____

Improvements
- ➢ _____
- ➢ _____
- ➢ _____

Expenses:
- ➢ _____
- ➢ _____
- ➢ _____
- ➢ _____

Notes:

"We are what we repeatedly do. Excellence, then, is not an act but a habit.
Aristotle

Monthly Seller Account Reconciliation

INCOME	Month:　　　　20____
Total Income from Sales:	$
Taxes collected by books:	$
Gross Profit (Total Sales minus Taxes)	$

EXPENSES	
Marketplaces Fees:	$
Cost of Goods Sold (COGS):	$
Shipping Expenses:	$
Storage/Rent:	$
Refunds:	$
Business Expenses (Apps, Software, etc.)	$
Other:	
Total Expenses for the Month:	$

PROFIT / LOSS	Month:　　　　20____
Net Profit = Gross Profit − Total Expenses	$
Net Profit Last Month:	$

Miles Deduction This Month: _____ Miles x $_____ / Per Mile =	$

Weekly Plan

Week: _____

MONDAY

TUESDAY

WED

THURSDAY

FRIDAY

SATURDAY

SUNDAY

Goals This Week
- ☐ Listing:_____
- ☐ Sourcing_____
- ☐ _____
- ☐ _____
- ☐ _____

Sales This Week
- ❖ _____
- ❖ _____
- ❖ _____

Improvements
- ➢ _____
- ➢ _____
- ➢ _____

Expenses:
- ➢ _____
- ➢ _____
- ➢ _____
- ➢ _____

Notes:

"There is nothing permanent except change."
Heraclitus

Weekly Plan

Week: _____

MONDAY

TUESDAY

WED

THURSDAY

FRIDAY

SATURDAY

SUNDAY

Goals This Week
- ❏ Listing:_____
- ❏ Sourcing_____
- ❏ _____
- ❏ _____
- ❏ _____

Sales This Week
- ❖ _____
- ❖ _____
- ❖ _____

Improvements
- ➢ _____
- ➢ _____
- ➢ _____

Expenses:
- ➢ _____
- ➢ _____
- ➢ _____
- ➢ _____

Notes:

When you want wisdom and insight as badly as you want to breathe, it is then you shall have it.
Socrates

Weekly Plan

Week: _____

MONDAY

TUESDAY

WED

THURSDAY

FRIDAY

SATURDAY

SUNDAY

Goals This Week

- ❏ Listing:_____
- ❏ Sourcing_____
- ❏ _____
- ❏ _____
- ❏ _____

Sales This Week

- ❖ _____
- ❖ _____
- ❖ _____

Improvements

- ➢ _____
- ➢ _____
- ➢ _____

Expenses:

- ➢ _____
- ➢ _____
- ➢ _____
- ➢ _____

Notes:

Thinking: the talking of the soul with itself.
Plato

Weekly Plan

Week: _____

MONDAY

TUESDAY

WED

THURSDAY

FRIDAY

SATURDAY

SUNDAY

Goals This Week

- ☐ Listing:_____
- ☐ Sourcing_____
- ☐ _____
- ☐ _____
- ☐ _____

Sales This Week

- ❖ _____
- ❖ _____
- ❖ _____

Improvements

- ➢ _____
- ➢ _____
- ➢ _____

Expenses:

- ➢ _____
- ➢ _____
- ➢ _____
- ➢ _____

Notes:

The secret of happiness, you see, is not found in seeking more but in developing the capacity to enjoy less.
Socrates

Monthly Seller Account Reconciliation

INCOME	Month:　　　　20____
Total Income from Sales:	$
Taxes collected by books:	$
Gross Profit (Total Sales minus Taxes)	$
EXPENSES	
Marketplaces Fees:	$
Cost of Goods Sold (COGS):	$
Shipping Expenses:	$
Storage/Rent:	$
Refunds:	$
Business Expenses (Apps, Software, etc.)	$
Other:	
Total Expenses for the Month:	$
PROFIT / LOSS	Month:　　　　20____
Net Profit = Gross Profit − Total Expenses	$
Net Profit Last Month:	$

Miles Deduction This Month: _____ Miles x $_____ / Per Mile =	$

Weekly Plan

Week: _____

Goals This Week

- ☐ Listing:_____
- ☐ Sourcing_____
- ☐ _____
- ☐ _____
- ☐ _____

Sales This Week

- ❖ _____
- ❖ _____
- ❖ _____

Improvements

- ➢ _____
- ➢ _____
- ➢ _____

Expenses:

- ➢ _____
- ➢ _____
- ➢ _____
- ➢ _____

MONDAY

TUESDAY

WED

THURSDAY

FRIDAY

SATURDAY

SUNDAY

Notes:

It's not what happens to you, but how you react to it that matters.
Epictetus

Weekly Plan

Week: _____

MONDAY

TUESDAY

WED

THURSDAY

FRIDAY

SATURDAY

SUNDAY

Goals This Week
- ☐ Listing:_____
- ☐ Sourcing_____
- ☐ _____
- ☐ _____
- ☐ _____

Sales This Week
- ❖ _____
- ❖ _____
- ❖ _____

Improvements
- ➢ _____
- ➢ _____
- ➢ _____

Expenses:
- ➢ _____
- ➢ _____
- ➢ _____
- ➢ _____

Notes:

"In three words I can sum up everything I've learned about life: it goes on."
Robert Frost

Weekly Plan

Week: _____

MONDAY

TUESDAY

WED

THURSDAY

FRIDAY

SATURDAY

SUNDAY

Goals This Week
- ❏ Listing:_____
- ❏ Sourcing_____
- ❏ _____
- ❏ _____
- ❏ _____

Sales This Week
- ❖ _____
- ❖ _____
- ❖ _____

Improvements
- ➢ _____
- ➢ _____
- ➢ _____

Expenses:
- ➢ _____
- ➢ _____
- ➢ _____
- ➢ _____

Notes:

"I have not failed. I've just found 10,000 ways that won't work."
Thomas Edison

Weekly Plan

Week: _____

MONDAY	
TUESDAY	
WED	
THURSDAY	
FRIDAY	
SATURDAY	
SUNDAY	

Goals This Week

- ❑ Listing:_____
- ❑ Sourcing_____
- ❑ _____
- ❑ _____
- ❑ _____

Sales This Week

- ❖ _____
- ❖ _____
- ❖ _____

Improvements

- ➢ _____
- ➢ _____
- ➢ _____

Expenses:

- ➢ _____
- ➢ _____
- ➢ _____
- ➢ _____

Notes:

"A journey of a thousand miles begins with a single step."
Lao Tzu

Monthly Seller Account Reconciliation

INCOME	Month: 20___
Total Income from Sales:	$
Taxes collected by books:	$
Gross Profit (Total Sales minus Taxes)	$
EXPENSES	
Marketplaces Fees:	$
Cost of Goods Sold (COGS):	$
Shipping Expenses:	$
Storage/Rent:	$
Refunds:	$
Business Expenses (Apps, Software, etc.)	$
Other:	
Total Expenses for the Month:	$

PROFIT / LOSS	Month: 20___
Net Profit = Gross Profit – Total Expenses	$
Net Profit Last Month:	$

Miles Deduction This Month: _____ Miles x $_____ / Per Mile =	$

Weekly Plan

Week: _____

Monday

Tuesday

Wed

Thursday

Friday

Saturday

Sunday

Goals This Week
- ☐ Listing:_____
- ☐ Sourcing_____
- ☐ _____
- ☐ _____
- ☐ _____

Sales This Week
- ❖ _____
- ❖ _____
- ❖ _____

Improvements
- ➤ _____
- ➤ _____
- ➤ _____

Expenses:
- ➤ _____
- ➤ _____
- ➤ _____
- ➤ _____

Notes:

"The greatest glory in living lies not in never falling, but in rising every time we fall."
Nelson Mandela

Weekly Plan

Week: _____

MONDAY

TUESDAY

WED

THURSDAY

FRIDAY

SATURDAY

SUNDAY

Goals This Week

- ☐ Listing:_____
- ☐ Sourcing_____
- ☐ _____
- ☐ _____
- ☐ _____

Sales This Week

- ❖ _____
- ❖ _____
- ❖ _____

Improvements

- ➢ _____
- ➢ _____
- ➢ _____

Expenses:

- ➢ _____
- ➢ _____
- ➢ _____
- ➢ _____

Notes:

"The best preparation for tomorrow is doing your best today."
H. Jackson Brown Jr.

Weekly Plan

Week: _____

MONDAY

TUESDAY

WED

THURSDAY

FRIDAY

SATURDAY

SUNDAY

Goals This Week

- ❑ Listing:_____
- ❑ Sourcing_____
- ❑ _____
- ❑ _____
- ❑ _____

Sales This Week

- ❖ _____
- ❖ _____
- ❖ _____

Improvements

- ➢ _____
- ➢ _____
- ➢ _____

Expenses:

- ➢ _____
- ➢ _____
- ➢ _____
- ➢ _____

Notes:

"It does not matter how slowly you go as long as you do not stop."
Confucius

Weekly Plan

Week: _____

MONDAY

TUESDAY

WED

THURSDAY

FRIDAY

SATURDAY

SUNDAY

Goals This Week
- ☐ Listing:_____
- ☐ Sourcing_____
- ☐ _____
- ☐ _____
- ☐ _____

Sales This Week
- ❖ _____
- ❖ _____
- ❖ _____

Improvements
- ➢ _____
- ➢ _____
- ➢ _____

Expenses:
- ➢ _____
- ➢ _____
- ➢ _____
- ➢ _____

Notes:

"To succeed in life, you need two things: ignorance and confidence."
— Mark Twain

Monthly Seller Account Reconciliation

INCOME	Month: 20____
Total Income from Sales:	$
Taxes collected by books:	$
Gross Profit (Total Sales minus Taxes)	$

EXPENSES	
Marketplaces Fees:	$
Cost of Goods Sold (COGS):	$
Shipping Expenses:	$
Storage/Rent:	$
Refunds:	$
Business Expenses (Apps, Software, etc.)	$
Other:	
Total Expenses for the Month:	$

PROFIT / LOSS	Month: 20____
Net Profit = Gross Profit – Total Expenses	$
Net Profit Last Month:	$

Miles Deduction This Month: _____ Miles x $_____ / Per Mile =	$

Weekly Plan

Week: _____

MONDAY	
TUESDAY	
WED	
THURSDAY	
FRIDAY	
SATURDAY	
SUNDAY	

Goals This Week

- ☐ Listing:_____
- ☐ Sourcing_____
- ☐ _____
- ☐ _____
- ☐ _____

Sales This Week

- ❖ _____
- ❖ _____
- ❖ _____

Improvements

- ➢ _____
- ➢ _____
- ➢ _____

Expenses:

- ➢ _____
- ➢ _____
- ➢ _____
- ➢ _____

Notes:

"Do not wait for leaders; do it alone, person to person."
Mother Teresa

Weekly Plan

Week: _____

MONDAY

TUESDAY

WED

THURSDAY

FRIDAY

SATURDAY

SUNDAY

Goals This Week

- ❑ Listing:_____
- ❑ Sourcing_____
- ❑ _____
- ❑ _____
- ❑ _____

Sales This Week

- ❖ _____
- ❖ _____
- ❖ _____

Improvements

- ➤ _____
- ➤ _____
- ➤ _____

Expenses:

- ➤ _____
- ➤ _____
- ➤ _____
- ➤ _____

Notes:

"The purpose of life is not to be happy. It is to be useful, to be honorable, to be compassionate, to have it make some difference that you have lived and lived well."
Ralph Waldo Emerson

Weekly Plan

Week: _____

MONDAY

TUESDAY

WED

THURSDAY

FRIDAY

SATURDAY

SUNDAY

Goals This Week
- ☐ Listing:_____
- ☐ Sourcing_____
- ☐ _____
- ☐ _____
- ☐ _____

Sales This Week
- ❖ _____
- ❖ _____
- ❖ _____

Improvements
- ➢ _____
- ➢ _____
- ➢ _____

Expenses:
- ➢ _____
- ➢ _____
- ➢ _____
- ➢ _____

Notes:

"In the middle of every difficulty lies opportunity."
Albert Einstein

Weekly Plan

Week: _____

MONDAY

TUESDAY

WED

THURSDAY

FRIDAY

SATURDAY

SUNDAY

Goals This Week

- ❏ Listing:_____
- ❏ Sourcing_____
- ❏ _____
- ❏ _____
- ❏ _____

Sales This Week

- ❖ _____
- ❖ _____
- ❖ _____

Improvements

- ➢ _____
- ➢ _____
- ➢ _____

Expenses:

- ➢ _____
- ➢ _____
- ➢ _____
- ➢ _____

Notes:

"Believe you can and you're halfway there."
Theodore Roosevelt

Monthly Seller Account Reconciliation

INCOME	Month: 20___
Total Income from Sales:	$
Taxes collected by books:	$
Gross Profit (Total Sales minus Taxes)	$

EXPENSES	
Marketplaces Fees:	$
Cost of Goods Sold (COGS):	$
Shipping Expenses:	$
Storage/Rent:	$
Refunds:	$
Business Expenses (Apps, Software, etc.)	$
Other:	
Total Expenses for the Month:	$

PROFIT / LOSS	Month: 20___
Net Profit = Gross Profit – Total Expenses	$
Net Profit Last Month:	$

Miles Deduction This Month: _____ Miles x $_____ / Per Mile =	$

Weekly Plan

Week: _____

MONDAY	
TUESDAY	
WED	
THURSDAY	
FRIDAY	
SATURDAY	
SUNDAY	

Goals This Week

- ☐ Listing:_____
- ☐ Sourcing_____
- ☐ _____
- ☐ _____
- ☐ _____

Sales This Week

- ❖ _____
- ❖ _____
- ❖ _____

Improvements

- ➢ _____
- ➢ _____
- ➢ _____

Expenses:

- ➢ _____
- ➢ _____
- ➢ _____
- ➢ _____

Notes:

"Success is not the key to happiness. Happiness is the key to success. If you love what you are doing, you will be successful."
Albert Schweitzer

Weekly Plan

Week: _____

MONDAY

TUESDAY

WED

THURSDAY

FRIDAY

SATURDAY

SUNDAY

Goals This Week

- ☐ Listing:_____
- ☐ Sourcing_____
- ☐ _____
- ☐ _____
- ☐ _____

Sales This Week

- ❖ _____
- ❖ _____
- ❖ _____

Improvements

- ➢ _____
- ➢ _____
- ➢ _____

Expenses:

- ➢ _____
- ➢ _____
- ➢ _____
- ➢ _____

Notes:

"The future belongs to those who believe in the beauty of their dreams."
Eleanor Roosevelt

Weekly Plan

Week: _____

MONDAY

TUESDAY

WED

THURSDAY

FRIDAY

SATURDAY

SUNDAY

Goals This Week
- ☐ Listing:_____
- ☐ Sourcing_____
- ☐ _____
- ☐ _____
- ☐ _____

Sales This Week
- ❖ _____
- ❖ _____
- ❖ _____

Improvements
- ➤ _____
- ➤ _____
- ➤ _____

Expenses:
- ➤ _____
- ➤ _____
- ➤ _____
- ➤ _____

Notes:

"If you want to achieve greatness, stop asking for permission."
Unknown

Weekly Plan

Week: _____

MONDAY	
TUESDAY	
WED	
THURSDAY	
FRIDAY	
SATURDAY	
SUNDAY	

Goals This Week

- ☐ Listing:_____
- ☐ Sourcing_____
- ☐ _____
- ☐ _____
- ☐ _____

Sales This Week

- ❖ _____
- ❖ _____
- ❖ _____

Improvements

- ➤ _____
- ➤ _____
- ➤ _____

Expenses:

- ➤ _____
- ➤ _____
- ➤ _____
- ➤ _____

Notes:

"It is not the strongest of the species that survive, nor the most intelligent, but the one most responsive to change." **–Charles Darwin**

Monthly Seller Account Reconciliation

INCOME	Month: 20___
Total Income from Sales:	$
Taxes collected by books:	$
Gross Profit (Total Sales minus Taxes)	$

EXPENSES	
Marketplaces Fees:	$
Cost of Goods Sold (COGS):	$
Shipping Expenses:	$
Storage/Rent:	$
Refunds:	$
Business Expenses (Apps, Software, etc.)	$
Other:	
Total Expenses for the Month:	$

PROFIT / LOSS	Month: 20___
Net Profit = Gross Profit – Total Expenses	$
Net Profit Last Month:	$

Miles Deduction This Month: _____ Miles x $_____ / Per Mile =	$

Weekly Plan

Week: _____

MONDAY

TUESDAY

WED

THURSDAY

FRIDAY

SATURDAY

SUNDAY

Goals This Week
- ☐ Listing:_____
- ☐ Sourcing_____
- ☐ _____
- ☐ _____
- ☐ _____

Sales This Week
- ❖ _____
- ❖ _____
- ❖ _____

Improvements
- ➤ _____
- ➤ _____
- ➤ _____

Expenses:
- ➤ _____
- ➤ _____
- ➤ _____
- ➤ _____

Notes:

"We are what we repeatedly do. Excellence, then, is not an act but a habit."
Aristotle

Weekly Plan

Week: _____

MONDAY

TUESDAY

WED

THURSDAY

FRIDAY

SATURDAY

SUNDAY

Goals This Week
- ☐ Listing:_____
- ☐ Sourcing_____
- ☐ _____
- ☐ _____
- ☐ _____

Sales This Week
- ❖ _____
- ❖ _____
- ❖ _____

Improvements
- ➢ _____
- ➢ _____
- ➢ _____

Expenses:
- ➢ _____
- ➢ _____
- ➢ _____
- ➢ _____

Notes:

"In the middle of difficulty lies opportunity."
Albert Einstein

Weekly Plan

Week: _____

MONDAY	
TUESDAY	
WED	
THURSDAY	
FRIDAY	
SATURDAY	
SUNDAY	

Goals This Week

- ❏ Listing:_____
- ❏ Sourcing_____
- ❏ _____
- ❏ _____
- ❏ _____

Sales This Week

- ❖ _____
- ❖ _____
- ❖ _____

Improvements

- ➢ _____
- ➢ _____
- ➢ _____

Expenses:

- ➢ _____
- ➢ _____
- ➢ _____
- ➢ _____

Notes:

The happiness of men consists in life.
And life is in labor.
Leo Tolstoy

Weekly Plan

Week: _____

MONDAY

TUESDAY

WED

THURSDAY

FRIDAY

SATURDAY

SUNDAY

Goals This Week
- ☐ Listing:_____
- ☐ Sourcing_____
- ☐ _____
- ☐ _____
- ☐ _____

Sales This Week
- ❖ _____
- ❖ _____
- ❖ _____

Improvements
- ➢ _____
- ➢ _____
- ➢ _____

Expenses:
- ➢ _____
- ➢ _____
- ➢ _____
- ➢ _____

Notes:

"To do for the world more than the world does for you, that is Success."
Henry Ford

Monthly Seller Account Reconciliation

INCOME	Month: 20___
Total Income from Sales:	$
Taxes collected by books:	$
Gross Profit (Total Sales minus Taxes)	$

EXPENSES	
Marketplaces Fees:	$
Cost of Goods Sold (COGS):	$
Shipping Expenses:	$
Storage/Rent:	$
Refunds:	$
Business Expenses (Apps, Software, etc.)	$
Other:	
Total Expenses for the Month:	$

PROFIT / LOSS	Month: 20___
Net Profit = Gross Profit − Total Expenses	$
Net Profit Last Month:	$

Miles Deduction This Month: _____ Miles x $_____ / Per Mile =	$

Weekly Plan

Week: _____

MONDAY

TUESDAY

WED

THURSDAY

FRIDAY

SATURDAY

SUNDAY

Goals This Week
- ❏ Listing:_____
- ❏ Sourcing_____
- ❏ _____
- ❏ _____
- ❏ _____

Sales This Week
- ❖ _____
- ❖ _____
- ❖ _____

Improvements
- ➢ _____
- ➢ _____
- ➢ _____

Expenses:
- ➢ _____
- ➢ _____
- ➢ _____
- ➢ _____

Notes:

*"To climb steep hills
Requires a slow pace at first."*
William Shakespeare

Weekly Plan

Week: _____

MONDAY	
TUESDAY	
WED	
THURSDAY	
FRIDAY	
SATURDAY	
SUNDAY	

Goals This Week
- ❏ Listing:_____
- ❏ Sourcing_____
- ❏ _____
- ❏ _____
- ❏ _____

Sales This Week
- ❖ _____
- ❖ _____
- ❖ _____

Improvements
- ➢ _____
- ➢ _____
- ➢ _____

Expenses:
- ➢ _____
- ➢ _____
- ➢ _____
- ➢ _____

Notes:

The secret of success is constancy of purpose.
Benjamin Disraeli

Weekly Plan

Week: _____

MONDAY

TUESDAY

WED

THURSDAY

FRIDAY

SATURDAY

SUNDAY

Goals This Week
- ❑ Listing:_____
- ❑ Sourcing_____
- ❑ _____
- ❑ _____
- ❑ _____

Sales This Week
- ❖ _____
- ❖ _____
- ❖ _____

Improvements
- ➢ _____
- ➢ _____
- ➢ _____

Expenses:
- ➢ _____
- ➢ _____
- ➢ _____
- ➢ _____

Notes:

"It is hard to fail, but it is worse never to have tried to succeed."
Theodore Roosevelt

Weekly Plan

Week: _____

MONDAY

TUESDAY

WED

THURSDAY

FRIDAY

SATURDAY

SUNDAY

Goals This Week
- ☐ Listing:_____
- ☐ Sourcing_____
- ☐ _____
- ☐ _____
- ☐ _____

Sales This Week
- ❖ _____
- ❖ _____
- ❖ _____

Improvements
- ➢ _____
- ➢ _____
- ➢ _____

Expenses:
- ➢ _____
- ➢ _____
- ➢ _____
- ➢ _____

Notes:

"The mind is everything. What you think you become."
Buddah

Monthly Seller Account Reconciliation

INCOME	Month: 20___
Total Income from Sales:	$
Taxes collected by books:	$
Gross Profit (Total Sales minus Taxes)	$

EXPENSES	
Marketplaces Fees:	$
Cost of Goods Sold (COGS):	$
Shipping Expenses:	$
Storage/Rent:	$
Refunds:	$
Business Expenses (Apps, Software, etc.)	$
Other:	
Total Expenses for the Month:	$

PROFIT / LOSS	Month: 20___
Net Profit = Gross Profit − Total Expenses	$
Net Profit Last Month:	$

Miles Deduction This Month: _____ Miles x $_____ / Per Mile =	$

Weekly Plan

Week: _____

MONDAY

TUESDAY

WED

THURSDAY

FRIDAY

SATURDAY

SUNDAY

Goals This Week

- ☐ Listing:_____
- ☐ Sourcing_____
- ☐ _____
- ☐ _____
- ☐ _____

Sales This Week

- ❖ _____
- ❖ _____
- ❖ _____

Improvements

- ➢ _____
- ➢ _____
- ➢ _____

Expenses:

- ➢ _____
- ➢ _____
- ➢ _____
- ➢ _____

Notes:

"Our greatest glory is not in never falling, but in rising every time we fall."
Confucius

Weekly Plan

Week: _____

MONDAY	
TUESDAY	
WED	
THURSDAY	
FRIDAY	
SATURDAY	
SUNDAY	

Goals This Week

- ❏ Listing:_____
- ❏ Sourcing_____
- ❏ _____
- ❏ _____
- ❏ _____

Sales This Week

- ❖ _____
- ❖ _____
- ❖ _____

Improvements

- ➢ _____
- ➢ _____
- ➢ _____

Expenses:

- ➢ _____
- ➢ _____
- ➢ _____
- ➢ _____

Notes:

"It always seems impossible until it's done."
Nelson Mandela

Weekly Plan

Week: _____

MONDAY	
TUESDAY	
WED	
THURSDAY	
FRIDAY	
SATURDAY	
SUNDAY	

Goals This Week

- ☐ Listing:_____
- ☐ Sourcing_____
- ☐ _____
- ☐ _____
- ☐ _____

Sales This Week

- ❖ _____
- ❖ _____
- ❖ _____

Improvements

- ➢ _____
- ➢ _____
- ➢ _____

Expenses:

- ➢ _____
- ➢ _____
- ➢ _____
- ➢ _____

Notes:

"Success usually comes to those who are too busy to be looking for it."
– Henry David Thoreau (1817–1862)

Weekly Plan

Week: _____

MONDAY	
TUESDAY	
WED	
THURSDAY	
FRIDAY	
SATURDAY	
SUNDAY	

Goals This Week

- ☐ Listing:_____
- ☐ Sourcing_____
- ☐ _____
- ☐ _____
- ☐ _____

Sales This Week

- ❖ _____
- ❖ _____
- ❖ _____

Improvements

- ➢ _____
- ➢ _____
- ➢ _____

Expenses:

- ➢ _____
- ➢ _____
- ➢ _____
- ➢ _____

Notes:

"The dictionary is the only place where success comes before work." - Mark Twain

Monthly Seller Account Reconciliation

INCOME	Month: 20___
Total Income from Sales:	$
Taxes collected by books:	$
Gross Profit (Total Sales minus Taxes)	$

EXPENSES	
Marketplaces Fees:	$
Cost of Goods Sold (COGS):	$
Shipping Expenses:	$
Storage/Rent:	$
Refunds:	$
Business Expenses (Apps, Software, etc.)	$
Other:	
Total Expenses for the Month:	$

PROFIT / LOSS	Month: 20___
Net Profit = Gross Profit – Total Expenses	$
Net Profit Last Month:	$

Miles Deduction This Month: _____ Miles x $_____ / Per Mile =	$

Weekly Plan

Week: _____

MONDAY

TUESDAY

WED

THURSDAY

FRIDAY

SATURDAY

SUNDAY

Goals This Week
- ☐ Listing:_____
- ☐ Sourcing_____
- ☐ _____
- ☐ _____
- ☐ _____

Sales This Week
- ❖ _____
- ❖ _____
- ❖ _____

Improvements
- ➢ _____
- ➢ _____
- ➢ _____

Expenses:
- ➢ _____
- ➢ _____
- ➢ _____
- ➢ _____

Notes:

"The only way to do great work is to love what you do."
- Oscar Wilde

Weekly Plan

Week: _____

MONDAY

TUESDAY

WED

THURSDAY

FRIDAY

SATURDAY

SUNDAY

Goals This Week
- ☐ Listing:_____
- ☐ Sourcing_____
- ☐ _____
- ☐ _____
- ☐ _____

Sales This Week
- ❖ _____
- ❖ _____
- ❖ _____

Improvements
- ➢ _____
- ➢ _____
- ➢ _____

Expenses:
- ➢ _____
- ➢ _____
- ➢ _____
- ➢ _____

Notes:

"The world is a book, and those who do not travel read only a page."
– Saint Augustine

Weekly Plan

Week: _____

MONDAY

TUESDAY

WED

THURSDAY

FRIDAY

SATURDAY

SUNDAY

Goals This Week
- ☐ Listing:_____
- ☐ Sourcing_____
- ☐ _____
- ☐ _____
- ☐ _____

Sales This Week
- ❖ _____
- ❖ _____
- ❖ _____

Improvements
- ➢ _____
- ➢ _____
- ➢ _____

Expenses:
- ➢ _____
- ➢ _____
- ➢ _____
- ➢ _____

Notes:

"Great things are not done by impulse but by a series of small things brought together."
- Vincent van Gogh (1853–1890)

Weekly Plan

Week: _____

MONDAY	
TUESDAY	
WED	
THURSDAY	
FRIDAY	
SATURDAY	
SUNDAY	

Goals This Week

- ❑ Listing:_____
- ❑ Sourcing_____
- ❑ _____
- ❑ _____
- ❑ _____

Sales This Week

- ❖ _____
- ❖ _____
- ❖ _____

Improvements

- ➢ _____
- ➢ _____
- ➢ _____

Expenses:

- ➢ _____
- ➢ _____
- ➢ _____
- ➢ _____

Notes:

"Do not go where the path may lead,
go instead where there is no path
and leave a trail."
- **Ralph Waldo Emerson**

Monthly Seller Account Reconciliation

INCOME	Month: 20___
Total Income from Sales:	$
Taxes collected by books:	$
Gross Profit (Total Sales minus Taxes)	$

EXPENSES	
Marketplaces Fees:	$
Cost of Goods Sold (COGS):	$
Shipping Expenses:	$
Storage/Rent:	$
Refunds:	$
Business Expenses (Apps, Software, etc.)	$
Other:	
Total Expenses for the Month:	$

PROFIT / LOSS	Month: 20___
Net Profit = Gross Profit – Total Expenses	$
Net Profit Last Month:	$

Miles Deduction This Month: _____ Miles x $_____ / Per Mile =	$

Weekly Plan

Week: _____

MONDAY

TUESDAY

WED

THURSDAY

FRIDAY

SATURDAY

SUNDAY

Goals This Week

- ☐ Listing:_____
- ☐ Sourcing_____
- ☐ _____
- ☐ _____
- ☐ _____

Sales This Week

- ❖ _____
- ❖ _____
- ❖ _____

Improvements

- ➢ _____
- ➢ _____
- ➢ _____

Expenses:

- ➢ _____
- ➢ _____
- ➢ _____
- ➢ _____

Notes:

"It was the best of times, it was the worst of times."
- **Charles Dickens (1812–1870)**

Weekly Plan

Week: _____

MONDAY

TUESDAY

WED

THURSDAY

FRIDAY

SATURDAY

SUNDAY

Goals This Week
- ☐ Listing:_____
- ☐ Sourcing_____
- ☐ _____
- ☐ _____
- ☐ _____

Sales This Week
- ❖ _____
- ❖ _____
- ❖ _____

Improvements
- ➢ _____
- ➢ _____
- ➢ _____

Expenses:
- ➢ _____
- ➢ _____
- ➢ _____
- ➢ _____

Notes:

"The first step to wisdom is silence; the second is listening."
- Solomon ibn Gabirol

Weekly Plan

Week: _____

MONDAY

TUESDAY

WED

THURSDAY

FRIDAY

SATURDAY

SUNDAY

Goals This Week
- ☐ Listing:_____
- ☐ Sourcing_____
- ☐ _____
- ☐ _____
- ☐ _____

Sales This Week
- ❖ _____
- ❖ _____
- ❖ _____

Improvements
- ➢ _____
- ➢ _____
- ➢ _____

Expenses:
- ➢ _____
- ➢ _____
- ➢ _____
- ➢ _____

Notes:

"It is not what we take up, but what we give up, that makes us rich."
- Henry Ward Beecher

Weekly Plan

Week: _____

MONDAY

TUESDAY

WED

THURSDAY

FRIDAY

SATURDAY

SUNDAY

Goals This Week
- ☐ Listing:_____
- ☐ Sourcing_____
- ☐ _____
- ☐ _____
- ☐ _____

Sales This Week
- ❖ _____
- ❖ _____
- ❖ _____

Improvements
- ➢ _____
- ➢ _____
- ➢ _____

Expenses:
- ➢ _____
- ➢ _____
- ➢ _____
- ➢ _____

Notes:

"It is better to be hated for what you are than to be loved for what you are not."
- André Gide (1869–1951)

Monthly Seller Account Reconciliation

INCOME	Month: 20___
Total Income from Sales:	$
Taxes collected by books:	$
Gross Profit (Total Sales minus Taxes)	$

EXPENSES	
Marketplaces Fees:	$
Cost of Goods Sold (COGS):	$
Shipping Expenses:	$
Storage/Rent:	$
Refunds:	$
Business Expenses (Apps, Software, etc.)	$
Other:	
Total Expenses for the Month:	$

PROFIT / LOSS	Month: 20___
Net Profit = Gross Profit – Total Expenses	$
Net Profit Last Month:	$

Miles Deduction This Month: _____ Miles x $_____ / Per Mile =	$

Miles Tracker
Instructions

Disclaimer: These tips are, in no way, legal or financial advice. Always consult a tax professional before deducting this expense from your tax returns.

Efficiently tracking miles traveled for business purposes is crucial for accurate record-keeping and potential tax deductions. Here are some practical tips to streamline this process:

- In the Worksheet, write the trip's date and purpose (dropping off packages, sourcing, buying supplies, etc.)
- Include the odometer's initial and ending miles and the miles traveled. For example, if your car was marking 32500 miles at the beginning of your trip, and when you were done, it was 32525, you would have traveled 25 miles for your business trip. Log all this down in the space provided.
- Quick Tip: If that day I am going to multiple sourcing places (stores, liquidation garage sales, etc.), I usually map those locations on Google Maps, get the miles driven from my home, and write them down in the log as total miles driven for the day.

Set a Routine:
- Establish a routine for logging miles, whether it's at the end of each day or week. Consistency ensures no trips are overlooked and the information remains up-to-date.

Understand IRS Requirements:
- Familiarize yourself with IRS requirements regarding mileage deductions. As tax regulations may change, staying informed ensures you comply with current guidelines and maximize your eligible deductions.

Efficiently tracking business miles simplifies tax reporting and provides valuable insights into the operational costs associated with your business-related travel. By adopting these strategies, you can effectively manage this aspect of your financial record-keeping.

Current Mileage Rate: _____ per Mile
Current Year _____
Notes:
_____
_____
_____

Miles Tracker

Date	Business Purpose	Odometer Start:	Odometer End:	Total Miles
			Total:	

Miles Tracker

Date	Business Purpose	Odometer Start:	Odometer End:	Total Miles
			Total:	

Miles Tracker

Date	Business Purpose	Odometer Start:	Odometer End:	Total Miles
			Total:	

Miles Tracker

Date	Business Purpose	Odometer Start:	Odometer End:	Total Miles
			Total:	

Why Logging in returns are essential:

Returns and credits in your store can happen weeks and months after a transaction. That is why the amount you get paid out and your sales sometimes do not match.

Why You Should Keep Track Of Your Returns:

Financial Accuracy:
- Keeping a record of returns is important for your reselling business. It helps you keep track of the money you made and the money you refunded for returned items. This way, you can have a better idea of your actual earnings.

Profitability Analysis:
- It's essential to keep track of returned products to figure out if your business is making a profit. By analyzing which items are returned the most, you can identify trends and make smarter decisions about what products to sell, how much to charge for them, and how to promote them.

Customer Insights:
- By looking at why customers return products, you can learn what they like and don't like. This can help you source better products, describe them better, and provide better customer service.

Inventory Management:
- Return logs play a crucial role in managing your inventory effectively. Knowing which items are returned allows you to update your inventory to know which items were returned.

Saving and printing a copy of your invoices every month will provide further records regarding your returns and credits. Please keep them in an envelope together with your receipts. When tax time comes, it will be easy to hand those to the accountant and store them away after tax season.

The author and its affiliates do not provide tax, legal, or accounting advice. This material has been prepared for informational purposes only and is not intended to provide, and should not be relied on for, tax, legal, or accounting advice. You should consult your tax, legal, and accounting advisors before engaging in any transaction.

Return Log

Date	Item:	Platform: (eBay, etc.)	Amount

Date from:_____ to _____ Total Returns | $_____

Return Log

Date	Item:	Platform: (eBay, etc.)	Amount

Date from:_____to _____Total Returns | $_____

Return Log

Date	Item:	Platform: (eBay, etc.)	Amount

Date from:_____to _____Total Returns | $_____

Cash Receipt Ledger

Date	Business Purpose/ Items	ATM/ CB*	Amount:

Use this ledger to keep track of garage sales, cash sales, ATM Withdrawals, and any other cash transactions out of your business account. *Cash Back

Cash Receipt Ledger

Date	Business Purpose/ Items	ATM/ CB*	Amount:

Use this ledger to keep track of garage sales, cash sales, ATM Withdrawals, and any other cash transactions out of your business account. *Cash Back

Cash Receipt Ledger

Date	Business Purpose/ Items	ATM/ CB*	Amount:

Use this ledger to keep track of garage sales, cash sales, ATM Withdrawals, and any other cash transactions out of your business account. *Cash Back

Cash Receipt Ledger

Date	Business Purpose/ Items	ATM/ CB*	Amount:

Use this ledger to keep track of garage sales, cash sales, ATM Withdrawals, and any other cash transactions out of your business account. *Cash Back

Cash Receipt Ledger

Date	Business Purpose/ Items	ATM/ CB*	Amount:

Use this ledger to keep track of garage sales, cash sales, ATM Withdrawals, and any other cash transactions out of your business account. *Cash Back

Business Expenses Log

Date:	Vendor:	Description:	Amount:
			$
		Total:	$

Used for expenses like gas, tolls, supplies, tools, software, etc.

Business Expenses Log

Date:	Vendor:	Description:	Amount:
			$
		Total:	$

Used for expenses like gas, tolls, supplies, tools, software, etc.

Business Expenses Log

Date:	Vendor:	Description:	Amount:
			$
		Total:	$

Used for expenses like gas, tolls, supplies, tools, software, etc.

Business Expenses Log

Date:	Vendor:	Description:	Amount:
			$
		Total:	$

Used for expenses like gas, tolls, supplies, tools, software, etc.

Cost of Goods Sold
Amount spent on inventory:

Date	Item Category:	Store	Payment Type	Amount:
			Total:	$_____

Cost of Goods Sold
Amount spent on inventory:

Date	Item Category:	Store	Payment Type	Amount:
			Total:	$_____

Cost of Goods Sold
Amount spent on inventory:

Date	Item Category:	Store	Payment Type	Amount:
			Total:	$_____

Cost of Goods Sold
Amount spent on inventory:

Date	Item Category:	Store	Payment Type	Amount:
			Total:	$_____

Cost of Goods Sold
Amount spent on inventory:

Date	Item Category:	Store	Payment Type	Amount:
			Total:	$_____

Sale Days Tracker Instructions

- It's a good idea to track the sale days at your local stores. That way, you can start predicting when the items you want will be on sale. Discount!

- This method is an approximate science. Stores know people do this; sometimes, they switch it up a bit.

- Do not get discouraged; keeping a record of sale days will keep you ahead of the game. Increasing your chances of getting fresh inventory at the lowest price.

- Try to create relationships in the places you go sourcing, even garage sales. You never know when an opportunity will come your way just by asking. Make sure you are polite and respectful when introducing yourself as a reseller. Just ask if there is anything else they want to get rid of and that you may buy. Get inventory before it hits the shelves, in bulk and at a discount.

- Keep the guide with you so that you can write down the sale details right after you leave the store. You will begin to track the sale days.

- Use this guide to plan your route and maximize your time. Time is money!

- Keep your cost of goods very low so you can have room to negotiate, increasing your chances of selling your items quicker and at a reasonable price.

Sale Days Tracker

Date:_____ Day:_____	Store:
Colors/Tags:	
What's on sale:	
Notes:	

Date:_____ Day:_____	Store:
Colors/Tags:	
What's on sale:	
Notes:	

Date:_____ Day:_____	Store:
Colors/Tags:	
What's on sale:	
Notes:	

Date:_____ Day:_____	Store:
Colors/Tags:	
What's on sale:	
Notes:	

Date:_____ Day:_____	Store:
Colors/Tags:	
What's on sale:	
Notes:	

Date:_____ Day:_____	Store:
Colors/Tags:	
What's on sale:	
Notes:	

Notes:

Sale Days Tracker

Date:_____ Day:_____	Store:
Colors/Tags:	
What's on sale:	
Notes:	

Date:_____ Day:_____	Store:
Colors/Tags:	
What's on sale:	
Notes:	

Date:_____ Day:_____	Store:
Colors/Tags:	
What's on sale:	
Notes:	

Date:_____ Day:_____	Store:
Colors/Tags:	
What's on sale:	
Notes:	

Date:_____ Day:_____	Store:
Colors/Tags:	
What's on sale:	
Notes:	

Date:_____ Day:_____	Store:
Colors/Tags:	
What's on sale:	
Notes:	

Notes:

BOLOS (Be on the lookout for):

This refers to trendy and high value items to look for when out sourcing. Pay attention to what people are wearing, commercials, movies, celebrities, etc.

"Opportunity is missed by most people because it is dressed in overalls and looks like work." **Thomas A. Edison**

BOLOS (Be on the lookout for):

This refers to trendy and high value items to look for when out sourcing. Pay attention to what people are wearing, commercials, movies, celebrities, etc.

"Opportunity is missed by most people because it is dressed in overalls and looks like work." **Thomas A. Edison**

Date:_____   Inventory Log

Brand:	Size:	Color:	Flaws:
Chest:	Inseam:	Condition:	Style:
Shoulder:	Hips:	Listed: PM __ EBY ___ MER___ Other:_____	Women:____Men:__ __ Kids:____ _
Sleeves:	Length:	Cost:	Loc: SKU#
Waist:	FR: BR:	Date Acqd:	Sold on:

Brand:	Size:	Color:	Flaws:
Chest:	Inseam:	Condition:	Style:
Shoulder:	Hips:	Listed: PM __ EBY ___ MER___ Other:_____	Women:____Men:__ __ Kids:____ _
Sleeves:	Length:	Cost:	Loc: SKU#
Waist:	FR: BR:	Date Acqd:	Sold on:

Brand:	Size:	Color:	Flaws:
Chest:	Inseam:	Condition:	Style:
Shoulder:	Hips:	Listed: PM __ EBY ___ MER___ Other:_____	Women:____Men:__ __ Kids:____ _
Sleeves:	Length:	Cost:	Loc: SKU#
Waist:	FR: BR:	Date Acqd:	Sold on:

Brand:	Size:	Color:	Flaws:
Chest:	Inseam:	Condition:	Style:
Shoulder:	Hips:	Listed: PM __ EBY ___ MER___ Other:_____	Women:____Men:__ __ Kids:____ _
Sleeves:	Length:	Cost:	Loc: SKU#
Waist:	FR: BR:	Date Acqd:	Sold on:

Brand:	Size:	Color:	Flaws:
Chest:	Inseam:	Condition:	Style:
Shoulder:	Hips:	Listed: PM __ EBY ___ MER___ Other:_____	Women:____Men:__ __ Kids:____ _
Sleeves:	Length:	Cost:	Loc: SKU#
Waist:	FR: BR:	Date Acqd:	Sold on:

Date:_____   Inventory Log

Brand:	Size:	Color:	Flaws:
Chest:	Inseam:	Condition:	Style:
Shoulder:	Hips:	Listed: PM __ EBY ___ MER___ Other:_____	Women:____Men:__ __ Kids:_____ _
Sleeves:	Length:	Cost:	Loc: SKU#
Waist:	FR: BR:	Date Acqd:	Sold on:

Brand:	Size:	Color:	Flaws:
Chest:	Inseam:	Condition:	Style:
Shoulder:	Hips:	Listed: PM __ EBY ___ MER___ Other:_____	Women:____Men:__ __ Kids:_____ _
Sleeves:	Length:	Cost:	Loc: SKU#
Waist:	FR: BR:	Date Acqd:	Sold on:

Brand:	Size:	Color:	Flaws:
Chest:	Inseam:	Condition:	Style:
Shoulder:	Hips:	Listed: PM __ EBY ___ MER___ Other:_____	Women:____Men:__ __ Kids:_____ _
Sleeves:	Length:	Cost:	Loc: SKU#
Waist:	FR: BR:	Date Acqd:	Sold on:

Brand:	Size:	Color:	Flaws:
Chest:	Inseam:	Condition:	Style:
Shoulder:	Hips:	Listed: PM __ EBY ___ MER___ Other:_____	Women:____Men:__ __ Kids:_____ _
Sleeves:	Length:	Cost:	Loc: SKU#
Waist:	FR: BR:	Date Acqd:	Sold on:

Brand:	Size:	Color:	Flaws:
Chest:	Inseam:	Condition:	Style:
Shoulder:	Hips:	Listed: PM __ EBY ___ MER___ Other:_____	Women:____Men:__ __ Kids:_____ _
Sleeves:	Length:	Cost:	Loc: SKU#
Waist:	FR: BR:	Date Acqd:	Sold on:

Date:_____   Inventory Log

Brand:	Size:	Color:	Flaws:
Chest:	Inseam:	Condition:	Style:
Shoulder:	Hips:	Listed: PM __ EBY ___ MER___ Other:_____	Women:____Men:__ __Kids:_____
Sleeves:	Length:	Cost:	Loc: SKU#
Waist:	FR: BR:	Date Acqd:	Sold on:

Brand:	Size:	Color:	Flaws:
Chest:	Inseam:	Condition:	Style:
Shoulder:	Hips:	Listed: PM __ EBY ___ MER___ Other:_____	Women:____Men:__ __Kids:_____
Sleeves:	Length:	Cost:	Loc: SKU#
Waist:	FR: BR:	Date Acqd:	Sold on:

Brand:	Size:	Color:	Flaws:
Chest:	Inseam:	Condition:	Style:
Shoulder:	Hips:	Listed: PM __ EBY ___ MER___ Other:_____	Women:____Men:__ __Kids:_____
Sleeves:	Length:	Cost:	Loc: SKU#
Waist:	FR: BR:	Date Acqd:	Sold on:

Brand:	Size:	Color:	Flaws:
Chest:	Inseam:	Condition:	Style:
Shoulder:	Hips:	Listed: PM __ EBY ___ MER___ Other:_____	Women:____Men:__ __Kids:_____
Sleeves:	Length:	Cost:	Loc: SKU#
Waist:	FR: BR:	Date Acqd:	Sold on:

Brand:	Size:	Color:	Flaws:
Chest:	Inseam:	Condition:	Style:
Shoulder:	Hips:	Listed: PM __ EBY ___ MER___ Other:_____	Women:____Men:__ __Kids:_____
Sleeves:	Length:	Cost:	Loc: SKU#
Waist:	FR: BR:	Date Acqd:	Sold on:

Date:_____   Inventory Log

Brand:	Size:	Color:	Flaws:
Chest:	Inseam:	Condition:	Style:
Shoulder:	Hips:	Listed: PM __ EBY ___ MER___ Other:_____	Women:____Men:__ Kids:_____
Sleeves:	Length:	Cost:	Loc: SKU#
Waist:	FR: BR:	Date Acqd:	Sold on:

Brand:	Size:	Color:	Flaws:
Chest:	Inseam:	Condition:	Style:
Shoulder:	Hips:	Listed: PM __ EBY ___ MER___ Other:_____	Women:____Men:__ Kids:_____
Sleeves:	Length:	Cost:	Loc: SKU#
Waist:	FR: BR:	Date Acqd:	Sold on:

Brand:	Size:	Color:	Flaws:
Chest:	Inseam:	Condition:	Style:
Shoulder:	Hips:	Listed: PM __ EBY ___ MER___ Other:_____	Women:____Men:__ Kids:_____
Sleeves:	Length:	Cost:	Loc: SKU#
Waist:	FR: BR:	Date Acqd:	Sold on:

Brand:	Size:	Color:	Flaws:
Chest:	Inseam:	Condition:	Style:
Shoulder:	Hips:	Listed: PM __ EBY ___ MER___ Other:_____	Women:____Men:__ Kids:_____
Sleeves:	Length:	Cost:	Loc: SKU#
Waist:	FR: BR:	Date Acqd:	Sold on:

Brand:	Size:	Color:	Flaws:
Chest:	Inseam:	Condition:	Style:
Shoulder:	Hips:	Listed: PM __ EBY ___ MER___ Other:_____	Women:____Men:__ Kids:_____
Sleeves:	Length:	Cost:	Loc: SKU#
Waist:	FR: BR:	Date Acqd:	Sold on:

Date:_____   Inventory Log

Brand:	Size:	Color:	Flaws:
Chest:	Inseam:	Condition:	Style:
Shoulder:	Hips:	Listed: PM __ EBY ___ MER___ Other:_____	Women:____Men:__ __ Kids:____ _
Sleeves:	Length:	Cost:	Loc: SKU#
Waist:	FR: BR:	Date Acqd:	Sold on:

Brand:	Size:	Color:	Flaws:
Chest:	Inseam:	Condition:	Style:
Shoulder:	Hips:	Listed: PM __ EBY ___ MER___ Other:_____	Women:____Men:__ __ Kids:____ _
Sleeves:	Length:	Cost:	Loc: SKU#
Waist:	FR: BR:	Date Acqd:	Sold on:

Brand:	Size:	Color:	Flaws:
Chest:	Inseam:	Condition:	Style:
Shoulder:	Hips:	Listed: PM __ EBY ___ MER___ Other:_____	Women:____Men:__ __ Kids:____ _
Sleeves:	Length:	Cost:	Loc: SKU#
Waist:	FR: BR:	Date Acqd:	Sold on:

Brand:	Size:	Color:	Flaws:
Chest:	Inseam:	Condition:	Style:
Shoulder:	Hips:	Listed: PM __ EBY ___ MER___ Other:_____	Women:____Men:__ __ Kids:____ _
Sleeves:	Length:	Cost:	Loc: SKU#
Waist:	FR: BR:	Date Acqd:	Sold on:

Brand:	Size:	Color:	Flaws:
Chest:	Inseam:	Condition:	Style:
Shoulder:	Hips:	Listed: PM __ EBY ___ MER___ Other:_____	Women:____Men:__ __ Kids:____ _
Sleeves:	Length:	Cost:	Loc: SKU#
Waist:	FR: BR:	Date Acqd:	Sold on:

Date:_____   Inventory Log

Brand:	Size:	Color:	Flaws:
Chest:	Inseam:	Condition:	Style:
Shoulder:	Hips:	Listed: PM __ EBY ___ MER___ Other:_____	Women:____Men:__ ___ Kids:_____ _
Sleeves:	Length:	Cost:	Loc: SKU#
Waist:	FR: BR:	Date Acqd:	Sold on:

Brand:	Size:	Color:	Flaws:
Chest:	Inseam:	Condition:	Style:
Shoulder:	Hips:	Listed: PM __ EBY ___ MER___ Other:_____	Women:____Men:__ ___ Kids:_____ _
Sleeves:	Length:	Cost:	Loc: SKU#
Waist:	FR: BR:	Date Acqd:	Sold on:

Brand:	Size:	Color:	Flaws:
Chest:	Inseam:	Condition:	Style:
Shoulder:	Hips:	Listed: PM __ EBY ___ MER___ Other:_____	Women:____Men:__ ___ Kids:_____ _
Sleeves:	Length:	Cost:	Loc: SKU#
Waist:	FR: BR:	Date Acqd:	Sold on:

Brand:	Size:	Color:	Flaws:
Chest:	Inseam:	Condition:	Style:
Shoulder:	Hips:	Listed: PM __ EBY ___ MER___ Other:_____	Women:____Men:__ ___ Kids:_____ _
Sleeves:	Length:	Cost:	Loc: SKU#
Waist:	FR: BR:	Date Acqd:	Sold on:

Brand:	Size:	Color:	Flaws:
Chest:	Inseam:	Condition:	Style:
Shoulder:	Hips:	Listed: PM __ EBY ___ MER___ Other:_____	Women:____Men:__ ___ Kids:_____ _
Sleeves:	Length:	Cost:	Loc: SKU#
Waist:	FR: BR:	Date Acqd:	Sold on:

Date:_____   Inventory Log

Brand:	Size:	Color:	Flaws:
Chest:	Inseam:	Condition:	Style:
Shoulder:	Hips:	Listed: PM __ EBY ___ MER___ Other:_____	Women:____Men:__ __ Kids:____ _
Sleeves:	Length:	Cost:	Loc: SKU#
Waist:	FR: BR:	Date Acqd:	Sold on:

Brand:	Size:	Color:	Flaws:
Chest:	Inseam:	Condition:	Style:
Shoulder:	Hips:	Listed: PM __ EBY ___ MER___ Other:_____	Women:____Men:__ __ Kids:____ _
Sleeves:	Length:	Cost:	Loc: SKU#
Waist:	FR: BR:	Date Acqd:	Sold on:

Brand:	Size:	Color:	Flaws:
Chest:	Inseam:	Condition:	Style:
Shoulder:	Hips:	Listed: PM __ EBY ___ MER___ Other:_____	Women:____Men:__ __ Kids:____ _
Sleeves:	Length:	Cost:	Loc: SKU#
Waist:	FR: BR:	Date Acqd:	Sold on:

Brand:	Size:	Color:	Flaws:
Chest:	Inseam:	Condition:	Style:
Shoulder:	Hips:	Listed: PM __ EBY ___ MER___ Other:_____	Women:____Men:__ __ Kids:____ _
Sleeves:	Length:	Cost:	Loc: SKU#
Waist:	FR: BR:	Date Acqd:	Sold on:

Brand:	Size:	Color:	Flaws:
Chest:	Inseam:	Condition:	Style:
Shoulder:	Hips:	Listed: PM __ EBY ___ MER___ Other:_____	Women:____Men:__ __ Kids:____ _
Sleeves:	Length:	Cost:	Loc: SKU#
Waist:	FR: BR:	Date Acqd:	Sold on:

Date:_____   Inventory Log

Brand:	Size:	Color:	Flaws:
Chest:	Inseam:	Condition:	Style:
Shoulder:	Hips:	Listed: PM __ EBY ___ MER___ Other:_____	Women:____Men:__ __ Kids:_____ _
Sleeves:	Length:	Cost:	Loc: SKU#
Waist:	FR: BR:	Date Acqd:	Sold on:

Brand:	Size:	Color:	Flaws:
Chest:	Inseam:	Condition:	Style:
Shoulder:	Hips:	Listed: PM __ EBY ___ MER___ Other:_____	Women:____Men:__ __ Kids:_____ _
Sleeves:	Length:	Cost:	Loc: SKU#
Waist:	FR: BR:	Date Acqd:	Sold on:

Brand:	Size:	Color:	Flaws:
Chest:	Inseam:	Condition:	Style:
Shoulder:	Hips:	Listed: PM __ EBY ___ MER___ Other:_____	Women:____Men:__ __ Kids:_____ _
Sleeves:	Length:	Cost:	Loc: SKU#
Waist:	FR: BR:	Date Acqd:	Sold on:

Brand:	Size:	Color:	Flaws:
Chest:	Inseam:	Condition:	Style:
Shoulder:	Hips:	Listed: PM __ EBY ___ MER___ Other:_____	Women:____Men:__ __ Kids:_____ _
Sleeves:	Length:	Cost:	Loc: SKU#
Waist:	FR: BR:	Date Acqd:	Sold on:

Brand:	Size:	Color:	Flaws:
Chest:	Inseam:	Condition:	Style:
Shoulder:	Hips:	Listed: PM __ EBY ___ MER___ Other:_____	Women:____Men:__ __ Kids:_____ _
Sleeves:	Length:	Cost:	Loc: SKU#
Waist:	FR: BR:	Date Acqd:	Sold on:

Date:_____   Inventory Log

Brand:	Size:	Color:	Flaws:
Chest:	Inseam:	Condition:	Style:
Shoulder:	Hips:	Listed: PM __ EBY ___ MER___ Other:_____	Women:____Men:__ __ Kids:_____
Sleeves:	Length:	Cost:	Loc: SKU#
Waist:	FR: BR:	Date Acqd:	Sold on:
Brand:	Size:	Color:	Flaws:
Chest:	Inseam:	Condition:	Style:
Shoulder:	Hips:	Listed: PM __ EBY ___ MER___ Other:_____	Women:____Men:__ __ Kids:_____
Sleeves:	Length:	Cost:	Loc: SKU#
Waist:	FR: BR:	Date Acqd:	Sold on:
Brand:	Size:	Color:	Flaws:
Chest:	Inseam:	Condition:	Style:
Shoulder:	Hips:	Listed: PM __ EBY ___ MER___ Other:_____	Women:____Men:__ __ Kids:_____
Sleeves:	Length:	Cost:	Loc: SKU#
Waist:	FR: BR:	Date Acqd:	Sold on:
Brand:	Size:	Color:	Flaws:
Chest:	Inseam:	Condition:	Style:
Shoulder:	Hips:	Listed: PM __ EBY ___ MER___ Other:_____	Women:____Men:__ __ Kids:_____
Sleeves:	Length:	Cost:	Loc: SKU#
Waist:	FR: BR:	Date Acqd:	Sold on:
Brand:	Size:	Color:	Flaws:
Chest:	Inseam:	Condition:	Style:
Shoulder:	Hips:	Listed: PM __ EBY ___ MER___ Other:_____	Women:____Men:__ __ Kids:_____
Sleeves:	Length:	Cost:	Loc: SKU#
Waist:	FR: BR:	Date Acqd:	Sold on:

Date:_____   Inventory Log

Brand:	Size:	Color:	Flaws:
Chest:	Inseam:	Condition:	Style:
Shoulder:	Hips:	Listed: PM __ EBY ___ MER___ Other:_____	Women:____Men:__ Kids:____
Sleeves:	Length:	Cost:	Loc: SKU#
Waist:	FR: BR:	Date Acqd:	Sold on:

Brand:	Size:	Color:	Flaws:
Chest:	Inseam:	Condition:	Style:
Shoulder:	Hips:	Listed: PM __ EBY ___ MER___ Other:_____	Women:____Men:__ Kids:____
Sleeves:	Length:	Cost:	Loc: SKU#
Waist:	FR: BR:	Date Acqd:	Sold on:

Brand:	Size:	Color:	Flaws:
Chest:	Inseam:	Condition:	Style:
Shoulder:	Hips:	Listed: PM __ EBY ___ MER___ Other:_____	Women:____Men:__ Kids:____
Sleeves:	Length:	Cost:	Loc: SKU#
Waist:	FR: BR:	Date Acqd:	Sold on:

Brand:	Size:	Color:	Flaws:
Chest:	Inseam:	Condition:	Style:
Shoulder:	Hips:	Listed: PM __ EBY ___ MER___ Other:_____	Women:____Men:__ Kids:____
Sleeves:	Length:	Cost:	Loc: SKU#
Waist:	FR: BR:	Date Acqd:	Sold on:

Brand:	Size:	Color:	Flaws:
Chest:	Inseam:	Condition:	Style:
Shoulder:	Hips:	Listed: PM __ EBY ___ MER___ Other:_____	Women:____Men:__ Kids:____
Sleeves:	Length:	Cost:	Loc: SKU#
Waist:	FR: BR:	Date Acqd:	Sold on:

Date:_____   Inventory Log

Brand:	Size:	Color:	Flaws:
Chest:	Inseam:	Condition:	Style:
Shoulder:	Hips:	Listed: PM __ EBY ___ MER___ Other:_____	Women:____Men:__ __ Kids:____ _
Sleeves:	Length:	Cost:	Loc: SKU#
Waist:	FR: BR:	Date Acqd:	Sold on:

Brand:	Size:	Color:	Flaws:
Chest:	Inseam:	Condition:	Style:
Shoulder:	Hips:	Listed: PM __ EBY ___ MER___ Other:_____	Women:____Men:__ __ Kids:____ _
Sleeves:	Length:	Cost:	Loc: SKU#
Waist:	FR: BR:	Date Acqd:	Sold on:

Brand:	Size:	Color:	Flaws:
Chest:	Inseam:	Condition:	Style:
Shoulder:	Hips:	Listed: PM __ EBY ___ MER___ Other:_____	Women:____Men:__ __ Kids:____ _
Sleeves:	Length:	Cost:	Loc: SKU#
Waist:	FR: BR:	Date Acqd:	Sold on:

Brand:	Size:	Color:	Flaws:
Chest:	Inseam:	Condition:	Style:
Shoulder:	Hips:	Listed: PM __ EBY ___ MER___ Other:_____	Women:____Men:__ __ Kids:____ _
Sleeves:	Length:	Cost:	Loc: SKU#
Waist:	FR: BR:	Date Acqd:	Sold on:

Brand:	Size:	Color:	Flaws:
Chest:	Inseam:	Condition:	Style:
Shoulder:	Hips:	Listed: PM __ EBY ___ MER___ Other:_____	Women:____Men:__ __ Kids:____ _
Sleeves:	Length:	Cost:	Loc: SKU#
Waist:	FR: BR:	Date Acqd:	Sold on:

Inventory Log

Date:_____

Brand:	Size:	Color:	Flaws:
Chest:	Inseam:	Condition:	Style:
Shoulder:	Hips:	Listed: PM __ EBY ___ MER___ Other:_____	Women:____Men:__ __ Kids:_____ _
Sleeves:	Length:	Cost:	Loc: SKU#
Waist:	FR: BR:	Date Acqd:	Sold on:

Brand:	Size:	Color:	Flaws:
Chest:	Inseam:	Condition:	Style:
Shoulder:	Hips:	Listed: PM __ EBY ___ MER___ Other:_____	Women:____Men:__ __ Kids:_____ _
Sleeves:	Length:	Cost:	Loc: SKU#
Waist:	FR: BR:	Date Acqd:	Sold on:

Brand:	Size:	Color:	Flaws:
Chest:	Inseam:	Condition:	Style:
Shoulder:	Hips:	Listed: PM __ EBY ___ MER___ Other:_____	Women:____Men:__ __ Kids:_____ _
Sleeves:	Length:	Cost:	Loc: SKU#
Waist:	FR: BR:	Date Acqd:	Sold on:

Brand:	Size:	Color:	Flaws:
Chest:	Inseam:	Condition:	Style:
Shoulder:	Hips:	Listed: PM __ EBY ___ MER___ Other:_____	Women:____Men:__ __ Kids:_____ _
Sleeves:	Length:	Cost:	Loc: SKU#
Waist:	FR: BR:	Date Acqd:	Sold on:

Brand:	Size:	Color:	Flaws:
Chest:	Inseam:	Condition:	Style:
Shoulder:	Hips:	Listed: PM __ EBY ___ MER___ Other:_____	Women:____Men:__ __ Kids:_____ _
Sleeves:	Length:	Cost:	Loc: SKU#
Waist:	FR: BR:	Date Acqd:	Sold on:

Date:_____   Inventory Log

Brand:	Size:	Color:	Flaws:
Chest:	Inseam:	Condition:	Style:
Shoulder:	Hips:	Listed: PM __ EBY ___ MER___ Other:_____	Women:____Men:__ __ Kids:_____ _
Sleeves:	Length:	Cost:	Loc: SKU#
Waist:	FR: BR:	Date Acqd:	Sold on:

Brand:	Size:	Color:	Flaws:
Chest:	Inseam:	Condition:	Style:
Shoulder:	Hips:	Listed: PM __ EBY ___ MER___ Other:_____	Women:____Men:__ __ Kids:_____ _
Sleeves:	Length:	Cost:	Loc: SKU#
Waist:	FR: BR:	Date Acqd:	Sold on:

Brand:	Size:	Color:	Flaws:
Chest:	Inseam:	Condition:	Style:
Shoulder:	Hips:	Listed: PM __ EBY ___ MER___ Other:_____	Women:____Men:__ __ Kids:_____ _
Sleeves:	Length:	Cost:	Loc: SKU#
Waist:	FR: BR:	Date Acqd:	Sold on:

Brand:	Size:	Color:	Flaws:
Chest:	Inseam:	Condition:	Style:
Shoulder:	Hips:	Listed: PM __ EBY ___ MER___ Other:_____	Women:____Men:__ __ Kids:_____ _
Sleeves:	Length:	Cost:	Loc: SKU#
Waist:	FR: BR:	Date Acqd:	Sold on:

Brand:	Size:	Color:	Flaws:
Chest:	Inseam:	Condition:	Style:
Shoulder:	Hips:	Listed: PM __ EBY ___ MER___ Other:_____	Women:____Men:__ __ Kids:_____ _
Sleeves:	Length:	Cost:	Loc: SKU#
Waist:	FR: BR:	Date Acqd:	Sold on:

Date:_____   Inventory Log

Brand:	Size:	Color:	Flaws:
Chest:	Inseam:	Condition:	Style:
Shoulder:	Hips:	Listed: PM __ EBY __ MER___ Other:_____	Women:____Men:__ __ Kids:____ _
Sleeves:	Length:	Cost:	Loc: SKU#
Waist:	FR: BR:	Date Acqd:	Sold on:

Brand:	Size:	Color:	Flaws:
Chest:	Inseam:	Condition:	Style:
Shoulder:	Hips:	Listed: PM __ EBY __ MER___ Other:_____	Women:____Men:__ __ Kids:____ _
Sleeves:	Length:	Cost:	Loc: SKU#
Waist:	FR: BR:	Date Acqd:	Sold on:

Brand:	Size:	Color:	Flaws:
Chest:	Inseam:	Condition:	Style:
Shoulder:	Hips:	Listed: PM __ EBY __ MER___ Other:_____	Women:____Men:__ __ Kids:____ _
Sleeves:	Length:	Cost:	Loc: SKU#
Waist:	FR: BR:	Date Acqd:	Sold on:

Brand:	Size:	Color:	Flaws:
Chest:	Inseam:	Condition:	Style:
Shoulder:	Hips:	Listed: PM __ EBY __ MER___ Other:_____	Women:____Men:__ __ Kids:____ _
Sleeves:	Length:	Cost:	Loc: SKU#
Waist:	FR: BR:	Date Acqd:	Sold on:

Brand:	Size:	Color:	Flaws:
Chest:	Inseam:	Condition:	Style:
Shoulder:	Hips:	Listed: PM __ EBY __ MER___ Other:_____	Women:____Men:__ __ Kids:____ _
Sleeves:	Length:	Cost:	Loc: SKU#
Waist:	FR: BR:	Date Acqd:	Sold on:

Date:_____   Inventory Log

Brand:	Size:	Color:	Flaws:
Chest:	Inseam:	Condition:	Style:
Shoulder:	Hips:	Listed: PM __ EBY __ MER___ Other:_____	Women:___Men:__ Kids:_____
Sleeves:	Length:	Cost:	Loc: SKU#
Waist:	FR: BR:	Date Acqd:	Sold on:

Brand:	Size:	Color:	Flaws:
Chest:	Inseam:	Condition:	Style:
Shoulder:	Hips:	Listed: PM __ EBY __ MER___ Other:_____	Women:___Men:__ Kids:_____
Sleeves:	Length:	Cost:	Loc: SKU#
Waist:	FR: BR:	Date Acqd:	Sold on:

Brand:	Size:	Color:	Flaws:
Chest:	Inseam:	Condition:	Style:
Shoulder:	Hips:	Listed: PM __ EBY __ MER___ Other:_____	Women:___Men:__ Kids:_____
Sleeves:	Length:	Cost:	Loc: SKU#
Waist:	FR: BR:	Date Acqd:	Sold on:

Brand:	Size:	Color:	Flaws:
Chest:	Inseam:	Condition:	Style:
Shoulder:	Hips:	Listed: PM __ EBY __ MER___ Other:_____	Women:___Men:__ Kids:_____
Sleeves:	Length:	Cost:	Loc: SKU#
Waist:	FR: BR:	Date Acqd:	Sold on:

Brand:	Size:	Color:	Flaws:
Chest:	Inseam:	Condition:	Style:
Shoulder:	Hips:	Listed: PM __ EBY __ MER___ Other:_____	Women:___Men:__ Kids:_____
Sleeves:	Length:	Cost:	Loc: SKU#
Waist:	FR: BR:	Date Acqd:	Sold on:

Date:_____   Inventory Log

Brand:	Size:	Color:	Flaws:
Chest:	Inseam:	Condition:	Style:
Shoulder:	Hips:	Listed: PM __ EBY ___ MER___ Other:_____	Women:____Men:__ __ Kids:_____ _
Sleeves:	Length:	Cost:	Loc: SKU#
Waist:	FR: BR:	Date Acqd:	Sold on:

Brand:	Size:	Color:	Flaws:
Chest:	Inseam:	Condition:	Style:
Shoulder:	Hips:	Listed: PM __ EBY ___ MER___ Other:_____	Women:____Men:__ __ Kids:_____ _
Sleeves:	Length:	Cost:	Loc: SKU#
Waist:	FR: BR:	Date Acqd:	Sold on:

Brand:	Size:	Color:	Flaws:
Chest:	Inseam:	Condition:	Style:
Shoulder:	Hips:	Listed: PM __ EBY ___ MER___ Other:_____	Women:____Men:__ __ Kids:_____ _
Sleeves:	Length:	Cost:	Loc: SKU#
Waist:	FR: BR:	Date Acqd:	Sold on:

Brand:	Size:	Color:	Flaws:
Chest:	Inseam:	Condition:	Style:
Shoulder:	Hips:	Listed: PM __ EBY ___ MER___ Other:_____	Women:____Men:__ __ Kids:_____ _
Sleeves:	Length:	Cost:	Loc: SKU#
Waist:	FR: BR:	Date Acqd:	Sold on:

Brand:	Size:	Color:	Flaws:
Chest:	Inseam:	Condition:	Style:
Shoulder:	Hips:	Listed: PM __ EBY ___ MER___ Other:_____	Women:____Men:__ __ Kids:_____ _
Sleeves:	Length:	Cost:	Loc: SKU#
Waist:	FR: BR:	Date Acqd:	Sold on:

Date:_____ **Inventory Log**

Brand:	Size:	Color:	Flaws:
Chest:	Inseam:	Condition:	Style:
Shoulder:	Hips:	Listed: PM __ EBY ___ MER___ Other:_____	Women:____Men:__ __ Kids:____ _
Sleeves:	Length:	Cost:	Loc: SKU#
Waist:	FR: BR:	Date Acqd:	Sold on:

Brand:	Size:	Color:	Flaws:
Chest:	Inseam:	Condition:	Style:
Shoulder:	Hips:	Listed: PM __ EBY ___ MER___ Other:_____	Women:____Men:__ __ Kids:____ _
Sleeves:	Length:	Cost:	Loc: SKU#
Waist:	FR: BR:	Date Acqd:	Sold on:

Brand:	Size:	Color:	Flaws:
Chest:	Inseam:	Condition:	Style:
Shoulder:	Hips:	Listed: PM __ EBY ___ MER___ Other:_____	Women:____Men:__ __ Kids:____ _
Sleeves:	Length:	Cost:	Loc: SKU#
Waist:	FR: BR:	Date Acqd:	Sold on:

Brand:	Size:	Color:	Flaws:
Chest:	Inseam:	Condition:	Style:
Shoulder:	Hips:	Listed: PM __ EBY ___ MER___ Other:_____	Women:____Men:__ __ Kids:____ _
Sleeves:	Length:	Cost:	Loc: SKU#
Waist:	FR: BR:	Date Acqd:	Sold on:

Brand:	Size:	Color:	Flaws:
Chest:	Inseam:	Condition:	Style:
Shoulder:	Hips:	Listed: PM __ EBY ___ MER___ Other:_____	Women:____Men:__ __ Kids:____ _
Sleeves:	Length:	Cost:	Loc: SKU#
Waist:	FR: BR:	Date Acqd:	Sold on:

Date:_____ Inventory Log

Brand:	Size:	Color:	Flaws:
Chest:	Inseam:	Condition:	Style:
Shoulder:	Hips:	Listed: PM __ EBY ___ MER___ Other:_____	Women:____Men:__ __ Kids:____ _
Sleeves:	Length:	Cost:	Loc: SKU#
Waist:	FR: BR:	Date Acqd:	Sold on:

Brand:	Size:	Color:	Flaws:
Chest:	Inseam:	Condition:	Style:
Shoulder:	Hips:	Listed: PM __ EBY ___ MER___ Other:_____	Women:____Men:__ __ Kids:____ _
Sleeves:	Length:	Cost:	Loc: SKU#
Waist:	FR: BR:	Date Acqd:	Sold on:

Brand:	Size:	Color:	Flaws:
Chest:	Inseam:	Condition:	Style:
Shoulder:	Hips:	Listed: PM __ EBY ___ MER___ Other:_____	Women:____Men:__ __ Kids:____ _
Sleeves:	Length:	Cost:	Loc: SKU#
Waist:	FR: BR:	Date Acqd:	Sold on:

Brand:	Size:	Color:	Flaws:
Chest:	Inseam:	Condition:	Style:
Shoulder:	Hips:	Listed: PM __ EBY ___ MER___ Other:_____	Women:____Men:__ __ Kids:____ _
Sleeves:	Length:	Cost:	Loc: SKU#
Waist:	FR: BR:	Date Acqd:	Sold on:

Brand:	Size:	Color:	Flaws:
Chest:	Inseam:	Condition:	Style:
Shoulder:	Hips:	Listed: PM __ EBY ___ MER___ Other:_____	Women:____Men:__ __ Kids:____ _
Sleeves:	Length:	Cost:	Loc: SKU#
Waist:	FR: BR:	Date Acqd:	Sold on:

Date:_____   Inventory Log

Brand:	Size:	Color:	Flaws:
Chest:	Inseam:	Condition:	Style:
Shoulder:	Hips:	Listed: PM __ EBY ___ MER___ Other:_____	Women:____Men:__ __ Kids:____ _
Sleeves:	Length:	Cost:	Loc: SKU#
Waist:	FR: BR:	Date Acqd:	Sold on:

Brand:	Size:	Color:	Flaws:
Chest:	Inseam:	Condition:	Style:
Shoulder:	Hips:	Listed: PM __ EBY ___ MER___ Other:_____	Women:____Men:__ __ Kids:____ _
Sleeves:	Length:	Cost:	Loc: SKU#
Waist:	FR: BR:	Date Acqd:	Sold on:

Brand:	Size:	Color:	Flaws:
Chest:	Inseam:	Condition:	Style:
Shoulder:	Hips:	Listed: PM __ EBY ___ MER___ Other:_____	Women:____Men:__ __ Kids:____ _
Sleeves:	Length:	Cost:	Loc: SKU#
Waist:	FR: BR:	Date Acqd:	Sold on:

Brand:	Size:	Color:	Flaws:
Chest:	Inseam:	Condition:	Style:
Shoulder:	Hips:	Listed: PM __ EBY ___ MER___ Other:_____	Women:____Men:__ __ Kids:____ _
Sleeves:	Length:	Cost:	Loc: SKU#
Waist:	FR: BR:	Date Acqd:	Sold on:

Brand:	Size:	Color:	Flaws:
Chest:	Inseam:	Condition:	Style:
Shoulder:	Hips:	Listed: PM __ EBY ___ MER___ Other:_____	Women:____Men:__ __ Kids:____ _
Sleeves:	Length:	Cost:	Loc: SKU#
Waist:	FR: BR:	Date Acqd:	Sold on:

Date:_____   Inventory Log

Brand:	Size:	Color:	Flaws:
Chest:	Inseam:	Condition:	Style:
Shoulder:	Hips:	Listed: PM __ EBY ___ MER___ Other:_____	Women:____Men:__ __ Kids:_____ _
Sleeves:	Length:	Cost:	Loc: SKU#
Waist:	FR: BR:	Date Acqd:	Sold on:

Brand:	Size:	Color:	Flaws:
Chest:	Inseam:	Condition:	Style:
Shoulder:	Hips:	Listed: PM __ EBY ___ MER___ Other:_____	Women:____Men:__ __ Kids:_____ _
Sleeves:	Length:	Cost:	Loc: SKU#
Waist:	FR: BR:	Date Acqd:	Sold on:

Brand:	Size:	Color:	Flaws:
Chest:	Inseam:	Condition:	Style:
Shoulder:	Hips:	Listed: PM __ EBY ___ MER___ Other:_____	Women:____Men:__ __ Kids:_____ _
Sleeves:	Length:	Cost:	Loc: SKU#
Waist:	FR: BR:	Date Acqd:	Sold on:

Brand:	Size:	Color:	Flaws:
Chest:	Inseam:	Condition:	Style:
Shoulder:	Hips:	Listed: PM __ EBY ___ MER___ Other:_____	Women:____Men:__ __ Kids:_____ _
Sleeves:	Length:	Cost:	Loc: SKU#
Waist:	FR: BR:	Date Acqd:	Sold on:

Brand:	Size:	Color:	Flaws:
Chest:	Inseam:	Condition:	Style:
Shoulder:	Hips:	Listed: PM __ EBY ___ MER___ Other:_____	Women:____Men:__ __ Kids:_____ _
Sleeves:	Length:	Cost:	Loc: SKU#
Waist:	FR: BR:	Date Acqd:	Sold on:

Date:_____   Inventory Log

Brand:	Size:	Color:	Flaws:
Chest:	Inseam:	Condition:	Style:
Shoulder:	Hips:	Listed: PM __ EBY ___ MER___ Other:_____	Women:____Men:__ __ Kids:_____ _
Sleeves:	Length:	Cost:	Loc: SKU#
Waist:	FR: BR:	Date Acqd:	Sold on:

Brand:	Size:	Color:	Flaws:
Chest:	Inseam:	Condition:	Style:
Shoulder:	Hips:	Listed: PM __ EBY ___ MER___ Other:_____	Women:____Men:__ __ Kids:_____ _
Sleeves:	Length:	Cost:	Loc: SKU#
Waist:	FR: BR:	Date Acqd:	Sold on:

Brand:	Size:	Color:	Flaws:
Chest:	Inseam:	Condition:	Style:
Shoulder:	Hips:	Listed: PM __ EBY ___ MER___ Other:_____	Women:____Men:__ __ Kids:_____ _
Sleeves:	Length:	Cost:	Loc: SKU#
Waist:	FR: BR:	Date Acqd:	Sold on:

Brand:	Size:	Color:	Flaws:
Chest:	Inseam:	Condition:	Style:
Shoulder:	Hips:	Listed: PM __ EBY ___ MER___ Other:_____	Women:____Men:__ __ Kids:_____ _
Sleeves:	Length:	Cost:	Loc: SKU#
Waist:	FR: BR:	Date Acqd:	Sold on:

Brand:	Size:	Color:	Flaws:
Chest:	Inseam:	Condition:	Style:
Shoulder:	Hips:	Listed: PM __ EBY ___ MER___ Other:_____	Women:____Men:__ __ Kids:_____ _
Sleeves:	Length:	Cost:	Loc: SKU#
Waist:	FR: BR:	Date Acqd:	Sold on:

Date:_____   Inventory Log

Brand:	Size:	Color:	Flaws:
Chest:	Inseam:	Condition:	Style:
Shoulder:	Hips:	Listed: PM __ EBY ___ MER___ Other:_____	Women:____Men:__ Kids:____
Sleeves:	Length:	Cost:	Loc: SKU#
Waist:	FR: BR:	Date Acqd:	Sold on:

Brand:	Size:	Color:	Flaws:
Chest:	Inseam:	Condition:	Style:
Shoulder:	Hips:	Listed: PM __ EBY ___ MER___ Other:_____	Women:____Men:__ Kids:____
Sleeves:	Length:	Cost:	Loc: SKU#
Waist:	FR: BR:	Date Acqd:	Sold on:

Brand:	Size:	Color:	Flaws:
Chest:	Inseam:	Condition:	Style:
Shoulder:	Hips:	Listed: PM __ EBY ___ MER___ Other:_____	Women:____Men:__ Kids:____
Sleeves:	Length:	Cost:	Loc: SKU#
Waist:	FR: BR:	Date Acqd:	Sold on:

Brand:	Size:	Color:	Flaws:
Chest:	Inseam:	Condition:	Style:
Shoulder:	Hips:	Listed: PM __ EBY ___ MER___ Other:_____	Women:____Men:__ Kids:____
Sleeves:	Length:	Cost:	Loc: SKU#
Waist:	FR: BR:	Date Acqd:	Sold on:

Brand:	Size:	Color:	Flaws:
Chest:	Inseam:	Condition:	Style:
Shoulder:	Hips:	Listed: PM __ EBY ___ MER___ Other:_____	Women:____Men:__ Kids:____
Sleeves:	Length:	Cost:	Loc: SKU#
Waist:	FR: BR:	Date Acqd:	Sold on:

Date:_____   Inventory Log

Brand:	Size:	Color:	Flaws:
Chest:	Inseam:	Condition:	Style:
Shoulder:	Hips:	Listed: PM __ EBY ___ MER___ Other:_____	Women:____Men:__ __ Kids:____ _
Sleeves:	Length:	Cost:	Loc: SKU#
Waist:	FR: BR:	Date Acqd:	Sold on:

Brand:	Size:	Color:	Flaws:
Chest:	Inseam:	Condition:	Style:
Shoulder:	Hips:	Listed: PM __ EBY ___ MER___ Other:_____	Women:____Men:__ __ Kids:____ _
Sleeves:	Length:	Cost:	Loc: SKU#
Waist:	FR: BR:	Date Acqd:	Sold on:

Brand:	Size:	Color:	Flaws:
Chest:	Inseam:	Condition:	Style:
Shoulder:	Hips:	Listed: PM __ EBY ___ MER___ Other:_____	Women:____Men:__ __ Kids:____ _
Sleeves:	Length:	Cost:	Loc: SKU#
Waist:	FR: BR:	Date Acqd:	Sold on:

Brand:	Size:	Color:	Flaws:
Chest:	Inseam:	Condition:	Style:
Shoulder:	Hips:	Listed: PM __ EBY ___ MER___ Other:_____	Women:____Men:__ __ Kids:____ _
Sleeves:	Length:	Cost:	Loc: SKU#
Waist:	FR: BR:	Date Acqd:	Sold on:

Brand:	Size:	Color:	Flaws:
Chest:	Inseam:	Condition:	Style:
Shoulder:	Hips:	Listed: PM __ EBY ___ MER___ Other:_____	Women:____Men:__ __ Kids:____ _
Sleeves:	Length:	Cost:	Loc: SKU#
Waist:	FR: BR:	Date Acqd:	Sold on:

Date:_____   Inventory Log

Brand:	Size:	Color:	Flaws:
Chest:	Inseam:	Condition:	Style:
Shoulder:	Hips:	Listed: PM __ EBY ___ MER___ Other:_____	Women:____Men:__ __ Kids:____ _
Sleeves:	Length:	Cost:	Loc: SKU#
Waist:	FR: BR:	Date Acqd:	Sold on:

Brand:	Size:	Color:	Flaws:
Chest:	Inseam:	Condition:	Style:
Shoulder:	Hips:	Listed: PM __ EBY ___ MER___ Other:_____	Women:____Men:__ __ Kids:____ _
Sleeves:	Length:	Cost:	Loc: SKU#
Waist:	FR: BR:	Date Acqd:	Sold on:

Brand:	Size:	Color:	Flaws:
Chest:	Inseam:	Condition:	Style:
Shoulder:	Hips:	Listed: PM __ EBY ___ MER___ Other:_____	Women:____Men:__ __ Kids:____ _
Sleeves:	Length:	Cost:	Loc: SKU#
Waist:	FR: BR:	Date Acqd:	Sold on:

Brand:	Size:	Color:	Flaws:
Chest:	Inseam:	Condition:	Style:
Shoulder:	Hips:	Listed: PM __ EBY ___ MER___ Other:_____	Women:____Men:__ __ Kids:____ _
Sleeves:	Length:	Cost:	Loc: SKU#
Waist:	FR: BR:	Date Acqd:	Sold on:

Brand:	Size:	Color:	Flaws:
Chest:	Inseam:	Condition:	Style:
Shoulder:	Hips:	Listed: PM __ EBY ___ MER___ Other:_____	Women:____Men:__ __ Kids:____ _
Sleeves:	Length:	Cost:	Loc: SKU#
Waist:	FR: BR:	Date Acqd:	Sold on:

Date:_____   Inventory Log

Brand:	Size:	Color:	Flaws:
Chest:	Inseam:	Condition:	Style:
Shoulder:	Hips:	Listed: PM __ EBY ___ MER___ Other:_____	Women:____ Men:__ __ Kids:____ _
Sleeves:	Length:	Cost:	Loc: SKU#
Waist:	FR: BR:	Date Acqd:	Sold on:

Brand:	Size:	Color:	Flaws:
Chest:	Inseam:	Condition:	Style:
Shoulder:	Hips:	Listed: PM __ EBY ___ MER___ Other:_____	Women:____ Men:__ __ Kids:____ _
Sleeves:	Length:	Cost:	Loc: SKU#
Waist:	FR: BR:	Date Acqd:	Sold on:

Brand:	Size:	Color:	Flaws:
Chest:	Inseam:	Condition:	Style:
Shoulder:	Hips:	Listed: PM __ EBY ___ MER___ Other:_____	Women:____ Men:__ __ Kids:____ _
Sleeves:	Length:	Cost:	Loc: SKU#
Waist:	FR: BR:	Date Acqd:	Sold on:

Brand:	Size:	Color:	Flaws:
Chest:	Inseam:	Condition:	Style:
Shoulder:	Hips:	Listed: PM __ EBY ___ MER___ Other:_____	Women:____ Men:__ __ Kids:____ _
Sleeves:	Length:	Cost:	Loc: SKU#
Waist:	FR: BR:	Date Acqd:	Sold on:

Brand:	Size:	Color:	Flaws:
Chest:	Inseam:	Condition:	Style:
Shoulder:	Hips:	Listed: PM __ EBY ___ MER___ Other:_____	Women:____ Men:__ __ Kids:____ _
Sleeves:	Length:	Cost:	Loc: SKU#
Waist:	FR: BR:	Date Acqd:	Sold on:

Date:_____   Inventory Log

Brand:	Size:	Color:	Flaws:
Chest:	Inseam:	Condition:	Style:
Shoulder:	Hips:	Listed: PM __ EBY ___ MER___ Other:_____	Women:____Men:__ __ Kids:_____ _
Sleeves:	Length:	Cost:	Loc: SKU#
Waist:	FR: BR:	Date Acqd:	Sold on:

Brand:	Size:	Color:	Flaws:
Chest:	Inseam:	Condition:	Style:
Shoulder:	Hips:	Listed: PM __ EBY ___ MER___ Other:_____	Women:____Men:__ __ Kids:_____ _
Sleeves:	Length:	Cost:	Loc: SKU#
Waist:	FR: BR:	Date Acqd:	Sold on:

Brand:	Size:	Color:	Flaws:
Chest:	Inseam:	Condition:	Style:
Shoulder:	Hips:	Listed: PM __ EBY ___ MER___ Other:_____	Women:____Men:__ __ Kids:_____ _
Sleeves:	Length:	Cost:	Loc: SKU#
Waist:	FR: BR:	Date Acqd:	Sold on:

Brand:	Size:	Color:	Flaws:
Chest:	Inseam:	Condition:	Style:
Shoulder:	Hips:	Listed: PM __ EBY ___ MER___ Other:_____	Women:____Men:__ __ Kids:_____ _
Sleeves:	Length:	Cost:	Loc: SKU#
Waist:	FR: BR:	Date Acqd:	Sold on:

Brand:	Size:	Color:	Flaws:
Chest:	Inseam:	Condition:	Style:
Shoulder:	Hips:	Listed: PM __ EBY ___ MER___ Other:_____	Women:____Men:__ __ Kids:_____ _
Sleeves:	Length:	Cost:	Loc: SKU#
Waist:	FR: BR:	Date Acqd:	Sold on:

Date:_____   Inventory Log

Brand:	Size:	Color:	Flaws:
Chest:	Inseam:	Condition:	Style:
Shoulder:	Hips:	Listed: PM ___ EBY ___ MER ___ Other: _____	Women: ____ Men: __ Kids: ____
Sleeves:	Length:	Cost:	Loc: SKU#
Waist:	FR: BR:	Date Acqd:	Sold on:

Brand:	Size:	Color:	Flaws:
Chest:	Inseam:	Condition:	Style:
Shoulder:	Hips:	Listed: PM ___ EBY ___ MER ___ Other: _____	Women: ____ Men: __ Kids: ____
Sleeves:	Length:	Cost:	Loc: SKU#
Waist:	FR: BR:	Date Acqd:	Sold on:

Brand:	Size:	Color:	Flaws:
Chest:	Inseam:	Condition:	Style:
Shoulder:	Hips:	Listed: PM ___ EBY ___ MER ___ Other: _____	Women: ____ Men: __ Kids: ____
Sleeves:	Length:	Cost:	Loc: SKU#
Waist:	FR: BR:	Date Acqd:	Sold on:

Brand:	Size:	Color:	Flaws:
Chest:	Inseam:	Condition:	Style:
Shoulder:	Hips:	Listed: PM ___ EBY ___ MER ___ Other: _____	Women: ____ Men: __ Kids: ____
Sleeves:	Length:	Cost:	Loc: SKU#
Waist:	FR: BR:	Date Acqd:	Sold on:

Brand:	Size:	Color:	Flaws:
Chest:	Inseam:	Condition:	Style:
Shoulder:	Hips:	Listed: PM ___ EBY ___ MER ___ Other: _____	Women: ____ Men: __ Kids: ____
Sleeves:	Length:	Cost:	Loc: SKU#
Waist:	FR: BR:	Date Acqd:	Sold on:

Date:_____   Inventory Log

Brand:	Size:	Color:	Flaws:
Chest:	Inseam:	Condition:	Style:
Shoulder:	Hips:	Listed: PM __ EBY ___ MER___ Other:_____	Women:____Men:__ Kids:____
Sleeves:	Length:	Cost:	Loc: SKU#
Waist:	FR: BR:	Date Acqd:	Sold on:

Brand:	Size:	Color:	Flaws:
Chest:	Inseam:	Condition:	Style:
Shoulder:	Hips:	Listed: PM __ EBY ___ MER___ Other:_____	Women:____Men:__ Kids:____
Sleeves:	Length:	Cost:	Loc: SKU#
Waist:	FR: BR:	Date Acqd:	Sold on:

Brand:	Size:	Color:	Flaws:
Chest:	Inseam:	Condition:	Style:
Shoulder:	Hips:	Listed: PM __ EBY ___ MER___ Other:_____	Women:____Men:__ Kids:____
Sleeves:	Length:	Cost:	Loc: SKU#
Waist:	FR: BR:	Date Acqd:	Sold on:

Brand:	Size:	Color:	Flaws:
Chest:	Inseam:	Condition:	Style:
Shoulder:	Hips:	Listed: PM __ EBY ___ MER___ Other:_____	Women:____Men:__ Kids:____
Sleeves:	Length:	Cost:	Loc: SKU#
Waist:	FR: BR:	Date Acqd:	Sold on:

Brand:	Size:	Color:	Flaws:
Chest:	Inseam:	Condition:	Style:
Shoulder:	Hips:	Listed: PM __ EBY ___ MER___ Other:_____	Women:____Men:__ Kids:____
Sleeves:	Length:	Cost:	Loc: SKU#
Waist:	FR: BR:	Date Acqd:	Sold on:

Date:_____   Inventory Log

Brand:	Size:	Color:	Flaws:
Chest:	Inseam:	Condition:	Style:
Shoulder:	Hips:	Listed: PM __ EBY ___ MER___ Other:_____	Women:____Men:__ Kids:____ _
Sleeves:	Length:	Cost:	Loc: SKU#
Waist:	FR: BR:	Date Acqd:	Sold on:

Brand:	Size:	Color:	Flaws:
Chest:	Inseam:	Condition:	Style:
Shoulder:	Hips:	Listed: PM __ EBY ___ MER___ Other:_____	Women:____Men:__ Kids:____ _
Sleeves:	Length:	Cost:	Loc: SKU#
Waist:	FR: BR:	Date Acqd:	Sold on:

Brand:	Size:	Color:	Flaws:
Chest:	Inseam:	Condition:	Style:
Shoulder:	Hips:	Listed: PM __ EBY ___ MER___ Other:_____	Women:____Men:__ Kids:____ _
Sleeves:	Length:	Cost:	Loc: SKU#
Waist:	FR: BR:	Date Acqd:	Sold on:

Brand:	Size:	Color:	Flaws:
Chest:	Inseam:	Condition:	Style:
Shoulder:	Hips:	Listed: PM __ EBY ___ MER___ Other:_____	Women:____Men:__ Kids:____ _
Sleeves:	Length:	Cost:	Loc: SKU#
Waist:	FR: BR:	Date Acqd:	Sold on:

Brand:	Size:	Color:	Flaws:
Chest:	Inseam:	Condition:	Style:
Shoulder:	Hips:	Listed: PM __ EBY ___ MER___ Other:_____	Women:____Men:__ Kids:____ _
Sleeves:	Length:	Cost:	Loc: SKU#
Waist:	FR: BR:	Date Acqd:	Sold on:

Date:_____   Inventory Log

Brand:	Size:	Color:	Flaws:
Chest:	Inseam:	Condition:	Style:
Shoulder:	Hips:	Listed: PM __ EBY ___ MER___ Other:_____	Women:____Men:__ __ Kids:_____ _
Sleeves:	Length:	Cost:	Loc: SKU#
Waist:	FR: BR:	Date Acqd:	Sold on:

Brand:	Size:	Color:	Flaws:
Chest:	Inseam:	Condition:	Style:
Shoulder:	Hips:	Listed: PM __ EBY ___ MER___ Other:_____	Women:____Men:__ __ Kids:_____ _
Sleeves:	Length:	Cost:	Loc: SKU#
Waist:	FR: BR:	Date Acqd:	Sold on:

Brand:	Size:	Color:	Flaws:
Chest:	Inseam:	Condition:	Style:
Shoulder:	Hips:	Listed: PM __ EBY ___ MER___ Other:_____	Women:____Men:__ __ Kids:_____ _
Sleeves:	Length:	Cost:	Loc: SKU#
Waist:	FR: BR:	Date Acqd:	Sold on:

Brand:	Size:	Color:	Flaws:
Chest:	Inseam:	Condition:	Style:
Shoulder:	Hips:	Listed: PM __ EBY ___ MER___ Other:_____	Women:____Men:__ __ Kids:_____ _
Sleeves:	Length:	Cost:	Loc: SKU#
Waist:	FR: BR:	Date Acqd:	Sold on:

Brand:	Size:	Color:	Flaws:
Chest:	Inseam:	Condition:	Style:
Shoulder:	Hips:	Listed: PM __ EBY ___ MER___ Other:_____	Women:____Men:__ __ Kids:_____ _
Sleeves:	Length:	Cost:	Loc: SKU#
Waist:	FR: BR:	Date Acqd:	Sold on:

Date:_____   Inventory Log

Brand:	Size:	Color:	Flaws:
Chest:	Inseam:	Condition:	Style:
Shoulder:	Hips:	Listed: PM __ EBY ___ MER___ Other:_____	Women:____ Men:__ __ Kids:____ _
Sleeves:	Length:	Cost:	Loc: SKU#
Waist:	FR: BR:	Date Acqd:	Sold on:

Brand:	Size:	Color:	Flaws:
Chest:	Inseam:	Condition:	Style:
Shoulder:	Hips:	Listed: PM __ EBY ___ MER___ Other:_____	Women:____ Men:__ __ Kids:____ _
Sleeves:	Length:	Cost:	Loc: SKU#
Waist:	FR: BR:	Date Acqd:	Sold on:

Brand:	Size:	Color:	Flaws:
Chest:	Inseam:	Condition:	Style:
Shoulder:	Hips:	Listed: PM __ EBY ___ MER___ Other:_____	Women:____ Men:__ __ Kids:____ _
Sleeves:	Length:	Cost:	Loc: SKU#
Waist:	FR: BR:	Date Acqd:	Sold on:

Brand:	Size:	Color:	Flaws:
Chest:	Inseam:	Condition:	Style:
Shoulder:	Hips:	Listed: PM __ EBY ___ MER___ Other:_____	Women:____ Men:__ __ Kids:____ _
Sleeves:	Length:	Cost:	Loc: SKU#
Waist:	FR: BR:	Date Acqd:	Sold on:

Brand:	Size:	Color:	Flaws:
Chest:	Inseam:	Condition:	Style:
Shoulder:	Hips:	Listed: PM __ EBY ___ MER___ Other:_____	Women:____ Men:__ __ Kids:____ _
Sleeves:	Length:	Cost:	Loc: SKU#
Waist:	FR: BR:	Date Acqd:	Sold on:

Date:_____   Inventory Log

Brand:	Size:	Color:	Flaws:
Chest:	Inseam:	Condition:	Style:
Shoulder:	Hips:	Listed: PM __ EBY ___ MER___ Other:_____	Women:____Men:__ Kids:_____
Sleeves:	Length:	Cost:	Loc: SKU#
Waist:	FR: BR:	Date Acqd:	Sold on:

Brand:	Size:	Color:	Flaws:
Chest:	Inseam:	Condition:	Style:
Shoulder:	Hips:	Listed: PM __ EBY ___ MER___ Other:_____	Women:____Men:__ Kids:_____
Sleeves:	Length:	Cost:	Loc: SKU#
Waist:	FR: BR:	Date Acqd:	Sold on:

Brand:	Size:	Color:	Flaws:
Chest:	Inseam:	Condition:	Style:
Shoulder:	Hips:	Listed: PM __ EBY ___ MER___ Other:_____	Women:____Men:__ Kids:_____
Sleeves:	Length:	Cost:	Loc: SKU#
Waist:	FR: BR:	Date Acqd:	Sold on:

Brand:	Size:	Color:	Flaws:
Chest:	Inseam:	Condition:	Style:
Shoulder:	Hips:	Listed: PM __ EBY ___ MER___ Other:_____	Women:____Men:__ Kids:_____
Sleeves:	Length:	Cost:	Loc: SKU#
Waist:	FR: BR:	Date Acqd:	Sold on:

Brand:	Size:	Color:	Flaws:
Chest:	Inseam:	Condition:	Style:
Shoulder:	Hips:	Listed: PM __ EBY ___ MER___ Other:_____	Women:____Men:__ Kids:_____
Sleeves:	Length:	Cost:	Loc: SKU#
Waist:	FR: BR:	Date Acqd:	Sold on:

Date:_____   Inventory Log

Brand:	Size:	Color:	Flaws:
Chest:	Inseam:	Condition:	Style:
Shoulder:	Hips:	Listed: PM ___ EBY ___ MER ___ Other:_____	Women:____ Men:__ Kids:_____
Sleeves:	Length:	Cost:	Loc: SKU#
Waist:	FR: BR:	Date Acqd:	Sold on:

Brand:	Size:	Color:	Flaws:
Chest:	Inseam:	Condition:	Style:
Shoulder:	Hips:	Listed: PM ___ EBY ___ MER ___ Other:_____	Women:____ Men:__ Kids:_____
Sleeves:	Length:	Cost:	Loc: SKU#
Waist:	FR: BR:	Date Acqd:	Sold on:

Brand:	Size:	Color:	Flaws:
Chest:	Inseam:	Condition:	Style:
Shoulder:	Hips:	Listed: PM ___ EBY ___ MER ___ Other:_____	Women:____ Men:__ Kids:_____
Sleeves:	Length:	Cost:	Loc: SKU#
Waist:	FR: BR:	Date Acqd:	Sold on:

Brand:	Size:	Color:	Flaws:
Chest:	Inseam:	Condition:	Style:
Shoulder:	Hips:	Listed: PM ___ EBY ___ MER ___ Other:_____	Women:____ Men:__ Kids:_____
Sleeves:	Length:	Cost:	Loc: SKU#
Waist:	FR: BR:	Date Acqd:	Sold on:

Brand:	Size:	Color:	Flaws:
Chest:	Inseam:	Condition:	Style:
Shoulder:	Hips:	Listed: PM ___ EBY ___ MER ___ Other:_____	Women:____ Men:__ Kids:_____
Sleeves:	Length:	Cost:	Loc: SKU#
Waist:	FR: BR:	Date Acqd:	Sold on:

Date:_____   Inventory Log

Brand:	Size:	Color:	Flaws:
Chest:	Inseam:	Condition:	Style:
Shoulder:	Hips:	Listed: PM __ EBY ___ MER___ Other:_____	Women:____Men:__ __ Kids:____ _
Sleeves:	Length:	Cost:	Loc: SKU#
Waist:	FR: BR:	Date Acqd:	Sold on:

Brand:	Size:	Color:	Flaws:
Chest:	Inseam:	Condition:	Style:
Shoulder:	Hips:	Listed: PM __ EBY ___ MER___ Other:_____	Women:____Men:__ __ Kids:____ _
Sleeves:	Length:	Cost:	Loc: SKU#
Waist:	FR: BR:	Date Acqd:	Sold on:

Brand:	Size:	Color:	Flaws:
Chest:	Inseam:	Condition:	Style:
Shoulder:	Hips:	Listed: PM __ EBY ___ MER___ Other:_____	Women:____Men:__ __ Kids:____ _
Sleeves:	Length:	Cost:	Loc: SKU#
Waist:	FR: BR:	Date Acqd:	Sold on:

Brand:	Size:	Color:	Flaws:
Chest:	Inseam:	Condition:	Style:
Shoulder:	Hips:	Listed: PM __ EBY ___ MER___ Other:_____	Women:____Men:__ __ Kids:____ _
Sleeves:	Length:	Cost:	Loc: SKU#
Waist:	FR: BR:	Date Acqd:	Sold on:

Brand:	Size:	Color:	Flaws:
Chest:	Inseam:	Condition:	Style:
Shoulder:	Hips:	Listed: PM __ EBY ___ MER___ Other:_____	Women:____Men:__ __ Kids:____ _
Sleeves:	Length:	Cost:	Loc: SKU#
Waist:	FR: BR:	Date Acqd:	Sold on:

Date:_____   Inventory Log

Brand:	Size:	Color:	Flaws:
Chest:	Inseam:	Condition:	Style:
Shoulder:	Hips:	Listed: PM __ EBY ___ MER___ Other:_____	Women:____Men:__ __ Kids:____ _
Sleeves:	Length:	Cost:	Loc: SKU#
Waist:	FR: BR:	Date Acqd:	Sold on:

Brand:	Size:	Color:	Flaws:
Chest:	Inseam:	Condition:	Style:
Shoulder:	Hips:	Listed: PM __ EBY ___ MER___ Other:_____	Women:____Men:__ __ Kids:____ _
Sleeves:	Length:	Cost:	Loc: SKU#
Waist:	FR: BR:	Date Acqd:	Sold on:

Brand:	Size:	Color:	Flaws:
Chest:	Inseam:	Condition:	Style:
Shoulder:	Hips:	Listed: PM __ EBY ___ MER___ Other:_____	Women:____Men:__ __ Kids:____ _
Sleeves:	Length:	Cost:	Loc: SKU#
Waist:	FR: BR:	Date Acqd:	Sold on:

Brand:	Size:	Color:	Flaws:
Chest:	Inseam:	Condition:	Style:
Shoulder:	Hips:	Listed: PM __ EBY ___ MER___ Other:_____	Women:____Men:__ __ Kids:____ _
Sleeves:	Length:	Cost:	Loc: SKU#
Waist:	FR: BR:	Date Acqd:	Sold on:

Brand:	Size:	Color:	Flaws:
Chest:	Inseam:	Condition:	Style:
Shoulder:	Hips:	Listed: PM __ EBY ___ MER___ Other:_____	Women:____Men:__ __ Kids:____ _
Sleeves:	Length:	Cost:	Loc: SKU#
Waist:	FR: BR:	Date Acqd:	Sold on:

Date:_____   Inventory Log

Brand:	Size:	Color:	Flaws:
Chest:	Inseam:	Condition:	Style:
Shoulder:	Hips:	Listed: PM __ EBY ___ MER___ Other:_____	Women:____Men:__ __ Kids:____ _
Sleeves:	Length:	Cost:	Loc: SKU#
Waist:	FR: BR:	Date Acqd:	Sold on:

Brand:	Size:	Color:	Flaws:
Chest:	Inseam:	Condition:	Style:
Shoulder:	Hips:	Listed: PM __ EBY ___ MER___ Other:_____	Women:____Men:__ __ Kids:____ _
Sleeves:	Length:	Cost:	Loc: SKU#
Waist:	FR: BR:	Date Acqd:	Sold on:

Brand:	Size:	Color:	Flaws:
Chest:	Inseam:	Condition:	Style:
Shoulder:	Hips:	Listed: PM __ EBY ___ MER___ Other:_____	Women:____Men:__ __ Kids:____ _
Sleeves:	Length:	Cost:	Loc: SKU#
Waist:	FR: BR:	Date Acqd:	Sold on:

Brand:	Size:	Color:	Flaws:
Chest:	Inseam:	Condition:	Style:
Shoulder:	Hips:	Listed: PM __ EBY ___ MER___ Other:_____	Women:____Men:__ __ Kids:____ _
Sleeves:	Length:	Cost:	Loc: SKU#
Waist:	FR: BR:	Date Acqd:	Sold on:

Brand:	Size:	Color:	Flaws:
Chest:	Inseam:	Condition:	Style:
Shoulder:	Hips:	Listed: PM __ EBY ___ MER___ Other:_____	Women:____Men:__ __ Kids:____ _
Sleeves:	Length:	Cost:	Loc: SKU#
Waist:	FR: BR:	Date Acqd:	Sold on:

Date:_____   Inventory Log

Brand:	Size:	Color:	Flaws:
Chest:	Inseam:	Condition:	Style:
Shoulder:	Hips:	Listed: PM __ EBY ___ MER___ Other:_____	Women:____Men:__ __ Kids:____ _
Sleeves:	Length:	Cost:	Loc: SKU#
Waist:	FR: BR:	Date Acqd:	Sold on:

Brand:	Size:	Color:	Flaws:
Chest:	Inseam:	Condition:	Style:
Shoulder:	Hips:	Listed: PM __ EBY ___ MER___ Other:_____	Women:____Men:__ __ Kids:____ _
Sleeves:	Length:	Cost:	Loc: SKU#
Waist:	FR: BR:	Date Acqd:	Sold on:

Brand:	Size:	Color:	Flaws:
Chest:	Inseam:	Condition:	Style:
Shoulder:	Hips:	Listed: PM __ EBY ___ MER___ Other:_____	Women:____Men:__ __ Kids:____ _
Sleeves:	Length:	Cost:	Loc: SKU#
Waist:	FR: BR:	Date Acqd:	Sold on:

Brand:	Size:	Color:	Flaws:
Chest:	Inseam:	Condition:	Style:
Shoulder:	Hips:	Listed: PM __ EBY ___ MER___ Other:_____	Women:____Men:__ __ Kids:____ _
Sleeves:	Length:	Cost:	Loc: SKU#
Waist:	FR: BR:	Date Acqd:	Sold on:

Brand:	Size:	Color:	Flaws:
Chest:	Inseam:	Condition:	Style:
Shoulder:	Hips:	Listed: PM __ EBY ___ MER___ Other:_____	Women:____Men:__ __ Kids:____ _
Sleeves:	Length:	Cost:	Loc: SKU#
Waist:	FR: BR:	Date Acqd:	Sold on:

Date:_____ Inventory Log

Brand:	Size:	Color:	Flaws:
Chest:	Inseam:	Condition:	Style:
Shoulder:	Hips:	Listed: PM __ EBY ___ MER___ Other:_____	Women:____Men:__ __ Kids:_____ _
Sleeves:	Length:	Cost:	Loc: SKU#
Waist:	FR: BR:	Date Acqd:	Sold on:

Brand:	Size:	Color:	Flaws:
Chest:	Inseam:	Condition:	Style:
Shoulder:	Hips:	Listed: PM __ EBY ___ MER___ Other:_____	Women:____Men:__ __ Kids:_____ _
Sleeves:	Length:	Cost:	Loc: SKU#
Waist:	FR: BR:	Date Acqd:	Sold on:

Brand:	Size:	Color:	Flaws:
Chest:	Inseam:	Condition:	Style:
Shoulder:	Hips:	Listed: PM __ EBY ___ MER___ Other:_____	Women:____Men:__ __ Kids:_____ _
Sleeves:	Length:	Cost:	Loc: SKU#
Waist:	FR: BR:	Date Acqd:	Sold on:

Brand:	Size:	Color:	Flaws:
Chest:	Inseam:	Condition:	Style:
Shoulder:	Hips:	Listed: PM __ EBY ___ MER___ Other:_____	Women:____Men:__ __ Kids:_____ _
Sleeves:	Length:	Cost:	Loc: SKU#
Waist:	FR: BR:	Date Acqd:	Sold on:

Brand:	Size:	Color:	Flaws:
Chest:	Inseam:	Condition:	Style:
Shoulder:	Hips:	Listed: PM __ EBY ___ MER___ Other:_____	Women:____Men:__ __ Kids:_____ _
Sleeves:	Length:	Cost:	Loc: SKU#
Waist:	FR: BR:	Date Acqd:	Sold on:

Date:_____   Inventory Log

Brand:	Size:	Color:	Flaws:
Chest:	Inseam:	Condition:	Style:
Shoulder:	Hips:	Listed: PM __ EBY ___ MER___ Other:_____	Women:____Men:__ __ Kids:_____ _
Sleeves:	Length:	Cost:	Loc: SKU#
Waist:	FR: BR:	Date Acqd:	Sold on:

Brand:	Size:	Color:	Flaws:
Chest:	Inseam:	Condition:	Style:
Shoulder:	Hips:	Listed: PM __ EBY ___ MER___ Other:_____	Women:____Men:__ __ Kids:_____ _
Sleeves:	Length:	Cost:	Loc: SKU#
Waist:	FR: BR:	Date Acqd:	Sold on:

Brand:	Size:	Color:	Flaws:
Chest:	Inseam:	Condition:	Style:
Shoulder:	Hips:	Listed: PM __ EBY ___ MER___ Other:_____	Women:____Men:__ __ Kids:_____ _
Sleeves:	Length:	Cost:	Loc: SKU#
Waist:	FR: BR:	Date Acqd:	Sold on:

Brand:	Size:	Color:	Flaws:
Chest:	Inseam:	Condition:	Style:
Shoulder:	Hips:	Listed: PM __ EBY ___ MER___ Other:_____	Women:____Men:__ __ Kids:_____ _
Sleeves:	Length:	Cost:	Loc: SKU#
Waist:	FR: BR:	Date Acqd:	Sold on:

Brand:	Size:	Color:	Flaws:
Chest:	Inseam:	Condition:	Style:
Shoulder:	Hips:	Listed: PM __ EBY ___ MER___ Other:_____	Women:____Men:__ __ Kids:_____ _
Sleeves:	Length:	Cost:	Loc: SKU#
Waist:	FR: BR:	Date Acqd:	Sold on:

Date:_____   Inventory Log

Brand:	Size:	Color:	Flaws:
Chest:	Inseam:	Condition:	Style:
Shoulder:	Hips:	Listed: PM __ EBY ___ MER___ Other:_____	Women:____Men:__ __ Kids:_____
Sleeves:	Length:	Cost:	Loc: SKU#
Waist:	FR: BR:	Date Acqd:	Sold on:

Brand:	Size:	Color:	Flaws:
Chest:	Inseam:	Condition:	Style:
Shoulder:	Hips:	Listed: PM __ EBY ___ MER___ Other:_____	Women:____Men:__ __ Kids:_____
Sleeves:	Length:	Cost:	Loc: SKU#
Waist:	FR: BR:	Date Acqd:	Sold on:

Brand:	Size:	Color:	Flaws:
Chest:	Inseam:	Condition:	Style:
Shoulder:	Hips:	Listed: PM __ EBY ___ MER___ Other:_____	Women:____Men:__ __ Kids:_____
Sleeves:	Length:	Cost:	Loc: SKU#
Waist:	FR: BR:	Date Acqd:	Sold on:

Brand:	Size:	Color:	Flaws:
Chest:	Inseam:	Condition:	Style:
Shoulder:	Hips:	Listed: PM __ EBY ___ MER___ Other:_____	Women:____Men:__ __ Kids:_____
Sleeves:	Length:	Cost:	Loc: SKU#
Waist:	FR: BR:	Date Acqd:	Sold on:

Brand:	Size:	Color:	Flaws:
Chest:	Inseam:	Condition:	Style:
Shoulder:	Hips:	Listed: PM __ EBY ___ MER___ Other:_____	Women:____Men:__ __ Kids:_____
Sleeves:	Length:	Cost:	Loc: SKU#
Waist:	FR: BR:	Date Acqd:	Sold on:

Date:_____   Inventory Log

Brand:	Size:	Color:	Flaws:
Chest:	Inseam:	Condition:	Style:
Shoulder:	Hips:	Listed: PM __ EBY ___ MER___ Other:_____	Women:____Men:__ __ Kids:____ _
Sleeves:	Length:	Cost:	Loc: SKU#
Waist:	FR: BR:	Date Acqd:	Sold on:

Brand:	Size:	Color:	Flaws:
Chest:	Inseam:	Condition:	Style:
Shoulder:	Hips:	Listed: PM __ EBY ___ MER___ Other:_____	Women:____Men:__ __ Kids:____ _
Sleeves:	Length:	Cost:	Loc: SKU#
Waist:	FR: BR:	Date Acqd:	Sold on:

Brand:	Size:	Color:	Flaws:
Chest:	Inseam:	Condition:	Style:
Shoulder:	Hips:	Listed: PM __ EBY ___ MER___ Other:_____	Women:____Men:__ __ Kids:____ _
Sleeves:	Length:	Cost:	Loc: SKU#
Waist:	FR: BR:	Date Acqd:	Sold on:

Brand:	Size:	Color:	Flaws:
Chest:	Inseam:	Condition:	Style:
Shoulder:	Hips:	Listed: PM __ EBY ___ MER___ Other:_____	Women:____Men:__ __ Kids:____ _
Sleeves:	Length:	Cost:	Loc: SKU#
Waist:	FR: BR:	Date Acqd:	Sold on:

Brand:	Size:	Color:	Flaws:
Chest:	Inseam:	Condition:	Style:
Shoulder:	Hips:	Listed: PM __ EBY ___ MER___ Other:_____	Women:____Men:__ __ Kids:____ _
Sleeves:	Length:	Cost:	Loc: SKU#
Waist:	FR: BR:	Date Acqd:	Sold on:

Date:_____   Inventory Log

Brand:	Size:	Color:	Flaws:
Chest:	Inseam:	Condition:	Style:
Shoulder:	Hips:	Listed: PM __ EBY ___ MER___ Other:_____	Women:____Men:__ __ Kids:____ _
Sleeves:	Length:	Cost:	Loc: SKU#
Waist:	FR: BR:	Date Acqd:	Sold on:

Brand:	Size:	Color:	Flaws:
Chest:	Inseam:	Condition:	Style:
Shoulder:	Hips:	Listed: PM __ EBY ___ MER___ Other:_____	Women:____Men:__ __ Kids:____ _
Sleeves:	Length:	Cost:	Loc: SKU#
Waist:	FR: BR:	Date Acqd:	Sold on:

Brand:	Size:	Color:	Flaws:
Chest:	Inseam:	Condition:	Style:
Shoulder:	Hips:	Listed: PM __ EBY ___ MER___ Other:_____	Women:____Men:__ __ Kids:____ _
Sleeves:	Length:	Cost:	Loc: SKU#
Waist:	FR: BR:	Date Acqd:	Sold on:

Brand:	Size:	Color:	Flaws:
Chest:	Inseam:	Condition:	Style:
Shoulder:	Hips:	Listed: PM __ EBY ___ MER___ Other:_____	Women:____Men:__ __ Kids:____ _
Sleeves:	Length:	Cost:	Loc: SKU#
Waist:	FR: BR:	Date Acqd:	Sold on:

Brand:	Size:	Color:	Flaws:
Chest:	Inseam:	Condition:	Style:
Shoulder:	Hips:	Listed: PM __ EBY ___ MER___ Other:_____	Women:____Men:__ __ Kids:____ _
Sleeves:	Length:	Cost:	Loc: SKU#
Waist:	FR: BR:	Date Acqd:	Sold on:

Date:_____   Inventory Log

Brand:	Size:	Color:	Flaws:
Chest:	Inseam:	Condition:	Style:
Shoulder:	Hips:	Listed: PM ___ EBY ___ MER ___ Other:_____	Women:____ Men:__ ___ Kids:_____ _
Sleeves:	Length:	Cost:	Loc: SKU#
Waist:	FR: BR:	Date Acqd:	Sold on:

Brand:	Size:	Color:	Flaws:
Chest:	Inseam:	Condition:	Style:
Shoulder:	Hips:	Listed: PM ___ EBY ___ MER ___ Other:_____	Women:____ Men:__ ___ Kids:_____ _
Sleeves:	Length:	Cost:	Loc: SKU#
Waist:	FR: BR:	Date Acqd:	Sold on:

Brand:	Size:	Color:	Flaws:
Chest:	Inseam:	Condition:	Style:
Shoulder:	Hips:	Listed: PM ___ EBY ___ MER ___ Other:_____	Women:____ Men:__ ___ Kids:_____ _
Sleeves:	Length:	Cost:	Loc: SKU#
Waist:	FR: BR:	Date Acqd:	Sold on:

Brand:	Size:	Color:	Flaws:
Chest:	Inseam:	Condition:	Style:
Shoulder:	Hips:	Listed: PM ___ EBY ___ MER ___ Other:_____	Women:____ Men:__ ___ Kids:_____ _
Sleeves:	Length:	Cost:	Loc: SKU#
Waist:	FR: BR:	Date Acqd:	Sold on:

Brand:	Size:	Color:	Flaws:
Chest:	Inseam:	Condition:	Style:
Shoulder:	Hips:	Listed: PM ___ EBY ___ MER ___ Other:_____	Women:____ Men:__ ___ Kids:_____ _
Sleeves:	Length:	Cost:	Loc: SKU#
Waist:	FR: BR:	Date Acqd:	Sold on:

Date:_____   Inventory Log

Brand:	Size:	Color:	Flaws:
Chest:	Inseam:	Condition:	Style:
Shoulder:	Hips:	Listed: PM __ EBY ___ MER___ Other:_____	Women:____Men:__ __ Kids:_____ _
Sleeves:	Length:	Cost:	Loc: SKU#
Waist:	FR: BR:	Date Acqd:	Sold on:

Brand:	Size:	Color:	Flaws:
Chest:	Inseam:	Condition:	Style:
Shoulder:	Hips:	Listed: PM __ EBY ___ MER___ Other:_____	Women:____Men:__ __ Kids:_____ _
Sleeves:	Length:	Cost:	Loc: SKU#
Waist:	FR: BR:	Date Acqd:	Sold on:

Brand:	Size:	Color:	Flaws:
Chest:	Inseam:	Condition:	Style:
Shoulder:	Hips:	Listed: PM __ EBY ___ MER___ Other:_____	Women:____Men:__ __ Kids:_____ _
Sleeves:	Length:	Cost:	Loc: SKU#
Waist:	FR: BR:	Date Acqd:	Sold on:

Brand:	Size:	Color:	Flaws:
Chest:	Inseam:	Condition:	Style:
Shoulder:	Hips:	Listed: PM __ EBY ___ MER___ Other:_____	Women:____Men:__ __ Kids:_____ _
Sleeves:	Length:	Cost:	Loc: SKU#
Waist:	FR: BR:	Date Acqd:	Sold on:

Brand:	Size:	Color:	Flaws:
Chest:	Inseam:	Condition:	Style:
Shoulder:	Hips:	Listed: PM __ EBY ___ MER___ Other:_____	Women:____Men:__ __ Kids:_____ _
Sleeves:	Length:	Cost:	Loc: SKU#
Waist:	FR: BR:	Date Acqd:	Sold on:

Date:_____   Inventory Log

Brand:	Size:	Color:	Flaws:
Chest:	Inseam:	Condition:	Style:
Shoulder:	Hips:	Listed: PM __ EBY ___ MER___ Other:_____	Women:____Men:__ __ Kids:_____ _
Sleeves:	Length:	Cost:	Loc: SKU#
Waist:	FR: BR:	Date Acqd:	Sold on:

Brand:	Size:	Color:	Flaws:
Chest:	Inseam:	Condition:	Style:
Shoulder:	Hips:	Listed: PM __ EBY ___ MER___ Other:_____	Women:____Men:__ __ Kids:_____ _
Sleeves:	Length:	Cost:	Loc: SKU#
Waist:	FR: BR:	Date Acqd:	Sold on:

Brand:	Size:	Color:	Flaws:
Chest:	Inseam:	Condition:	Style:
Shoulder:	Hips:	Listed: PM __ EBY ___ MER___ Other:_____	Women:____Men:__ __ Kids:_____ _
Sleeves:	Length:	Cost:	Loc: SKU#
Waist:	FR: BR:	Date Acqd:	Sold on:

Brand:	Size:	Color:	Flaws:
Chest:	Inseam:	Condition:	Style:
Shoulder:	Hips:	Listed: PM __ EBY ___ MER___ Other:_____	Women:____Men:__ __ Kids:_____ _
Sleeves:	Length:	Cost:	Loc: SKU#
Waist:	FR: BR:	Date Acqd:	Sold on:

Brand:	Size:	Color:	Flaws:
Chest:	Inseam:	Condition:	Style:
Shoulder:	Hips:	Listed: PM __ EBY ___ MER___ Other:_____	Women:____Men:__ __ Kids:_____ _
Sleeves:	Length:	Cost:	Loc: SKU#
Waist:	FR: BR:	Date Acqd:	Sold on:

We hope you enjoyed this book!

Would you please leave us a review on Amazon?

It would really help us out!

Feedback and comments from our readers really make our day!

Thank you!

Queen Thrift

Visit www.QueenThrift.com
For Freebies, Advance Copies, and More!